**one
less.
one
more.®**

10/16/14

To Patty,

We love you
and Always
follow your heart.

Fondly,

Debbie

# one less. one more.®

follow your heart.
be happy.
change slowly.

robbie vorhaus

*Storytelling, Inc.*

First Published by Storytelling Inc., 2014

Storytelling Inc.
Box 1619
Sag Harbor, New York 11963
www.storytelling.com

ISBN 978-0-9914658-0-4 (hardback)

First Edition
Printed in the United States of America
10 9 8 7 6 5 4 3 2 1


Text set in Palatino
Cover Design by Pearlfisher
Book Design by *the*BookDesigners
Printed and bound by Edwards Brothers Malloy

To the One in both less and more.
And to my beauties: Candace,
Connor, and Molly.
More and more.

*They must often change,*
*who would be constant in happiness or wisdom.*
– *Confucius*


*Happiness is the meaning and the purpose of life,*
*the whole aim and end of human existence.*
– *Aristotle*


*If one advances confidently in the*
*direction of his dreams,*
*and endeavors to live the life which he has imagined,*
*he will meet with a success unexpected*
*in common hours.*
– *Henry David Thoreau*, Walden

# Contents

**Author's Note**................................................1

**One Less, One More Daily Steps**...................3

**My Path**...................................................4

**One:** One Less. One More. ........................... 17

**Two:** Follow Your Heart ...............................25
   Less: Feeling Bad
   More: Feeling Good

**Three:** Believe.........................................53
   Less: Fear
   More: Awareness

**Four:** Prepare.........................................89
   Less: Ego
   More: Heart

**Five:** Commit .........................................115
   Less: Procrastination
   More: Proactivity

**Six:** Transition........................................141
   Less: Control
   More: Experience

**Seven:** Raising the Stakes ...................................... 171

    Less: Hoping, Wishing, Trying

    More: Doing

**Eight:** Crises – The Ultimate Challenge ................... 193

    Less: Blame

    More: Accountability

**Nine:** Choice .................................................... 221

    Less: Worse

    More: Better

**Ten:** Mastery ...................................................... 245

    Less: Perfection

    More: Practice

**The Daily One Less, One More Moment** ... 274

**Gratitude and Appreciation** .......................... 275

# Author's Note

Like a psychologist, financial advisor, or medical doctor, I am not at liberty to reveal or discuss my clients. Unless a client publicly reveals me as their advisor (and few do), I cannot discuss or even allude to my work for that person, government, sports team, corporation, or organization.

Consider this: You are powerful, rich and famous. Through a stupid mistake of your own, the malicious act of another, or what appears to be bad luck, your well-honed reputation and livelihood fall into jeopardy. You hire me to guide you through the crisis, and eventually, over time, regain your reputation and rebuild an even better, more abundant life.

Now imagine that before our work is completed, I start a self-promotion campaign on my website, in advertisements, in my books, and on TV appearances, all highlighting your crisis and publicizing our successful work together.

Although we've kept your crisis relatively quiet and out of the public eye, by marketing myself as your advisor I flame the fire of your mistakes and capitalize on your misfortune. How would you feel? Would you ever hire me again? Knowing that your emergency, major blunder, or indiscretion now lives forever in my promotional materials, what leader, famous person or country would ever hire me again? Not many, I assure you.

My advisory work demands strict privacy and intense secrecy. Often, until a crisis is over, my family doesn't know where I am, or for whom I'm working. Although this makes for interesting dinner conversation, it also requires my family, friends, and other clients' understanding, trust, and compassion.

Dear reader, I must now ask the same of you.

Throughout this book, all references to famous people are true and accurate. However, in many of the subsequent examples, when noted with an asterisk, I take the liberty to change names and pertinent details to protect my clients' security, reputation, and privacy.

Most of my clients are like you: good, solid, honest people, who by choice or chance, become faced with life-altering events and decisions. And they, like you, often just need a little help and support in making choices that will, ultimately, allow them to move beyond their past, and go on to follow their hearts and pursue their dreams, for a better, more fulfilling, and purposeful life.

Which is exactly why I wrote *One Less. One More.*

And finally, just as the familiar grocery store sign at the express line states, "10 items or less," instead of the grammatically correct, "10 items or fewer," I intentionally broke the prescriptive grammar rule of count versus mass nouns when I titled my book *One Less. One More.*

As *One Less* describes a singular concept, and when added to *One More*, becomes the first of a two-part, life-transforming formula, I am comfortable, as I hope you are, too, leaving the title as is: *One Less. One More.*

# One Less, One More
# Daily Steps

1. Start now.

2. Come present.

3. Consciously choose to follow your heart, be happy and change slowly.

4. Today, choose one less negative, resistant, or bad feeling, thought or action, and let it go. One Less.

5. Today, choose one more positive or good feeling, thought or action, and embrace it. One More.

6. Celebrate your progress.

7. Repeat tomorrow.

# My Path

**My mother, a Dutch holocaust survivor**, and my father, the son of Jewish New Yorkers, reluctantly moved to Levittown, Pennsylvania, a Philadelphia suburb, for a job my father never liked. My parents fueled their unhappiness with alcohol and fought constantly.

My father eventually left home, leaving me, the oldest of four children, torn between my mother's fear and anger at being a single parent, and the need to provide my younger brother, Bill, and two sisters, Lauren Adele and Carla, with emotional comfort and support. I struggled with my own severe dyslexia, and what is now known as Attention Deficit Hyperactivity Disorder (ADHD), all while attempting to earn some extra money for a family that, it seemed, never had enough.

I was also becoming a drug addict.

When I was twelve, our family doctor prescribed Valium for me telling my mother, "It should help calm him down." Originally approved in 1963, Valium, which is in the same classification as today's psychoactive drug Xanax, is a highly addictive drug used for *short-term* treatment of anxiety. My initial daily dose was a total of 15 mg – a little yellow pill, five mg, taken three times a day.

At thirteen, I became a paperboy for the *Bucks County Courier Times,* and at fifteen, I became a darkroom assistant in the paper's photography department. A year later, at sixteen, I got my first professional camera, a driver's license, a police scanner, and became a spot-news photographer, chasing ambulances and fire engines for the *Courier Times*.

At the same time, things were getting worse at home.

My parents attempted reconciling, creating a cauldron of abuse resulting in repeated police visits to our home. My parents finally separated for good, and my daily Valium dosage was increased to 25 mg.

I didn't have enough credits to graduate high school, and there was no money available for college. I eventually passed my high school equivalency test (the GED), after being physically forced from my home at seventeen.

Homeless for several months, I scraped together enough money for a small studio apartment, and continued working for the newspaper, along with additional part-time jobs, including the graveyard shifts at a local factory and a 7-Eleven.

Three years later, I moved to Des Moines, Iowa, married, and worked at a local radio station. By now, simply to function, I was taking a ridiculously high dosage of 50+ mg of Valium daily. Over the course of the next couple of years, I tried unsuccessfully to quit Valium, yet just reducing the dosage proved painful and disruptive. In order to function normally it was easier to stay addicted.

By twenty-three, my marriage was failing, and I began devouring every religious, spiritual and self-help book I could find: the Old and New Testament; the Hindu *Bhagavad Gita*; the *I-Ching*; Lao Tsu's *Tao Te Ching*; Shunryu Suzuki's *Zen Mind, Beginner's Mind*; Dr. Thomas Harris's *I'm OK - You're OK*; Ram Dass's *Be Here Now*; even Richard Bach's *Jonathan Livingston Seagull*.

I spent early morning hours in prayer and meditation, and, although in a constant Valium-induced fog, I soon came to feel like two people; one being an out-of-control drug-addict, and the other a conscious spirit, a soul completely untouched and unaffected by the drugs. I came to believe that if I wanted to quit my eleven-year Valium addiction, I just needed to shift my focus away from my twenty-three-year-old habituated mind and body, and instead, identify with my eternal, drug-free, and infinite heart; my spirit, my soul.

Against almost everyone's recommendations, and not really acknowledging the potential life-threatening risks, I chose to go cold turkey and quit Valium alone; a really bad and dangerous idea.

On a bitterly cold Friday morning, overlooking a sea of Iowa cornfields, in an apartment at the edge of West Des Moines, I stopped taking Valium.

By night I was a convulsive wreck, and by the next day I was completely out of my mind. Losing control of every bodily function but breath, I lived for days in my bathtub. The following weeks were excruciating, and although I could write volumes about my experiences kicking Valium, I choose not to. I honor every person that has ever experienced or attempted addiction recovery, and the horror of the following months will always remain a private reminder of my soul's exquisite strength and beauty.

Several months later, now clean and single, I moved to Kansas City, Missouri, to work at the NBC TV affiliate station, and then two years later I returned to New York

City to pursue my dream of working in network TV.

Without a college degree, it was difficult landing a full-time staff job, but with daily persistence, I was eventually hired at CBS News as a "per-diem," a daily contract worker with no health-care benefits.

On my first day, I was led through the maze of the CBS Broadcast Center on 57th Street, to meet my new boss, Dan Rather, the then managing director and anchor of *The CBS Evening News.*

"Where did you go to college?" Mr. Rather questioned me in his Texas drawl.

"Nowhere, sir," I said.

"How did you land a job here, among all these Harvard, Yale and Columbia grads?"

"Prayer, persistence, and good fortune, Mr. Rather," I replied.

"Well," Rather laughed, sticking out his big hand to shake mine, "that makes you my new best friend. Welcome to CBS News."

One advantage to being a contract worker, and not a staff employee, was the ability to change gears and pursue outside photojournalism projects.

In the spring of 1986, I was offered the unprecedented opportunity to spend one extraordinary year as an embedded journalist with a special group of New York City Police officers, in a little known unit simply called "Task Force."

Secretly headquartered in an old storage facility in East New York, Brooklyn, Task Force was an elite group of highly motivated undercover cops, hand picked to help reduce crime on New York City's subway and bus system.

Although the NYPD brass sanctioned my work, most cops believe journalists are never to be trusted, and I was no exception.

I was assigned to Team Seven, an eclectic group of both male and female cops on a career path to the coveted gold detective's shield. Anyone outside of these cops' very tightly knit circle was seen as an intrusion and potential threat to their ultimate goal of becoming a detective.

"It's not that we don't like you," one heavily tattooed, ex-Vietnam veteran said, "It's just, well, we don't like your kind."

I didn't give up, and by December my uniform consisted of construction boots, ratty, worn jeans and sweatshirts, along with a full beard, long hair pulled back in a ponytail and an old, smelly, Army combat fatigue jacket. Coupled with going several days without a shower, my disguise was complete, and I fit in perfectly down in "the hole," the subway.

Yet when my future wife, Candace, then the lovely Mary Candace Connors, moved in across the hall from my Upper Eastside apartment, her look of disdain when meeting me, her derelict neighbor, was apparent.

After a year, I finished my work with the NYPD, cut my hair, shaved, took a long hot shower, put on a suit, quickly became friends with Candace, and accepted an assignment in corporate communications at the CBS Television Network.

My office was at "Black Rock," CBS's big, black building

between 52$^{nd}$ and 53$^{rd}$ streets on the Avenue of the Americas; and in perfect synchronicity, Candace's office was a block away at the Radio City Music Hall building. From fall through the summer, for the entire next year, we walked to work together through Central Park, slowly falling in love. Engaged in August, almost one year to the day after we met, we were married in late July the following year, just shy of two years after our first date.

Candace went back to school and earned a fine arts degree at Parsons School of Design in New York, while also studying interior design at the Museum of Decorative Arts, part of the Louvre in Paris.

I left CBS TV, opened my consultancy, and immediately started signing influential business leaders, politicians, celebrities and high net-worth sports stars.

Almost five years after getting married, our son, Connor, was born, and two-and-a-half years later, daughter Molly was born.

Candace put her interior design business on hold to raise our children. I, on the other hand, wrestled with a growing business. Within a very short period of time, Vorhaus & Company was representing marquee clients, including Buick, Domino's Pizza, H.J. Heinz, Keebler, and Pfizer, and in 1997 we moved our offices to a much larger space at 53$^{rd}$ and Broadway, directly across the street from the Ed Sullivan Theatre, the home of the *Late Show* with David Letterman.

That summer, for fun when I traveled, I purchased a red Frisbee. On a whim, I began photographing people around the world holding my Frisbee, from Ireland to India, South Africa to the Dominican Republic, New York City to Los Angeles, France to Zimbabwe, and more. Each picture, with a different person holding the Frisbee, demonstrated a universal connection, and the work resonated with New York City's Bishop Patrick V. Ahern.

"Your Frisbee photography project is a sign of universal peace," Bishop Ahern told me one evening over dinner. "The Holy Father sees your photographic work as a peace offering to the world. Will you take his blessings?"

"The Pope?" I asked, incredulous. "I'm not even Catholic."

Bishop Ahern laughed. "You may be when this experience is over," he said.

Several weeks later I flew to Rome and, although in failing health, Pope John Paul II celebrated mass at the Vatican, and afterwards, I was escorted up to meet his Holiness.

I was expecting a quick, official "meet and greet," a short, perfunctory, mechanical greeting with a handshake, photographs, and a "thank you very much . . . next!" event.

Instead, I had a mystical, transformative experience, and my life has never been the same.

Approaching Pope John Paul II, I started feeling lighter, a little dizzy, and confused.

"How can this be?" I thought. "I work with famous people, don't often get star struck, I'm not Catholic, and yet my whole body is tingling."

With each footstep I felt like time was slowing down. Approaching the Pope, he appeared to be surrounded by radiant light, a subtle shining haze of vibrating luminosity.

As I got closer, I, too, began to radiate that same light, although mine felt less intense or clear.

The Pope reached out and took my hand. Instantly our lights combined. Together we stood inside this white, blue tinted, and pulsating, beautiful light. Although there were many people surrounding us, in that moment we were completely one, cocooned in a brilliant blanket of energetic unity.

To anyone watching, and as the picture on my wall shows, we stood talking as the Pope blessed me, as we continued holding hands.

Yet while we talked, on a deeper level, a door opened to my soul, and I began receiving incomprehensible amounts of the most beautiful light and love imaginable, a download of pure peace and harmony with no labels, boundaries, religion or division. This information I received had no attachments, I felt no emotion, and I was struck by the purity of this divine energy.

Once home, back in New York City, I felt compelled to do something different with my life, but what? Although I was not clear on the specifics of my future, my plan was simply to follow my heart. Easier said than done.

A reporter once asked a sculptor how he was able to produce such magnificent, realistic work, pointing, for example, to his current project, a galloping horse carved from stone.

The artist replied, "It's very simple. I take a rock and cut away everything that doesn't look like a horse."

Soon, I began cutting away aspects of my life that

didn't fit, such as toxic clients, employees, friends, and stock investments in companies not supporting our planet. I stopped eating foods with hydrogenated oils, and significantly cut down on red meat. I consciously stopped complaining and gossiping, and internally, I began eliminating negative thoughts related to possible doom and gloom events, while reducing my constant judgment of others. I took elevators less and the stairs more. Prone to embellishing, I consciously chose to exaggerate less, and instead, learned to become more understated.

I began training with a spiritual teacher, which carried over into both my personal and professional life. I was praying and meditating every day, walking the streets of New York City quietly performing random acts of kindness, spending more time with my family, and introducing a more conscious, spiritual aspect into my consulting practice.

Ego's a funny thing, and I thought I was doing okay. Actually, I thought I was doing great. I talked a good game, continued praying and meditating, and my clients were benefiting from my new direction. Two years later, though, my family took me on a Caribbean cruise for my birthday. Out at sea, one night before dinner, sitting on our balcony, the four of us started talking about our dreams and desires.

Molly went first, saying she wanted to spend more time in nature, work with horses and get a dog. Connor went next, saying he wanted more freedom, less stress, and the ability to ride his bike everywhere. Candace said she, too, wanted to live in nature, work with horses, and enjoy a more relaxed lifestyle. "I also want more of Dad!" she said in a tone that made the kids laugh, although I also heard her tinge of anger and frustration.

It was my turn and Molly hit me with the question, "Daddy, are you happy?"

My immediate reaction was, "Of course, baby-girl!" But they weren't buying it.

"Come on, Dad," the kids said. "Tell us the truth. Are you really happy?"

I dropped my veil and came clean. Yes, I liked helping and inspiring my clients, but, no, I did not enjoy the day-to-day challenges of running a mid-size public relations agency. I missed writing and photography, regretted the constant travel, and grew weary of missing important family events, like birthdays, fun holidays and concerts. As Candace would say, "You give your best to everyone else, with little left for our family and me." Ouch.

I love New York City, and always will, but I knew in my heart for our family to thrive, we needed another venue. Although I didn't admit this to the children, Candace knew I was beginning to develop high blood pressure, I was drinking too much, and our marriage was slowly falling apart.

I was clearly on a path, but this journey was not going to end well. I had convinced myself I was happy, although I was not. In truth, I felt like an empty shell.

Now what? My life's plan had been to build my business and sell it for a lot of money. My plan was to continue living on Park Avenue, have our children go to the best private schools in the world, and Candace and I would live happily ever after in financial bliss. On the outside, I was living the dream. On the inside, I was in danger of losing everything I held dear.

It was time to choose. Do I continue listening to the loud and competitive ego, with all the thoughts and fears in my head driving me even further away from my family, happiness and fulfillment, or do I make the biggest decision in my life and, as I decided after meeting the Pope, sincerely follow my heart?

When we came home from our cruise, everything looked different. I didn't have the same attachment to our New York City apartment, my business, and the children's schools. I also started our "What if . . .?" conversations. What if we run out of money? (Candace: "Then we start over.") What if we're not happy? (Candace: "As long as we have each other, we'll be fine.") What if closing my business and moving out of the city is a terrible mistake? (Candace: "Terrible mistakes lead to great discoveries. What's the worst that can happen?") What if I'm just one big phony? (Candace: "That's okay. I love you, the kids love you, and the Universe loves you. We're all phonies on some level. Go for it.")

Within a few months, I announced that I was closing my business to start a consulting practice. We sold our Park Avenue apartment (in one day!), and with the proceeds, paid off business and personal back taxes, loans and leases. We pulled the children from their world-class private schools, and moved to our small weekend home in Sag Harbor, New York. Less urban, more rural.

There's a terrific expression, "Bloom where you're

planted," and soon our family began to thrive. For the first time as a collective unit, we moved together with a rhythm just our own. Not perfect, of course, but even in our breakdowns we made breakthroughs, bringing us even closer together.

My health improved, as did our marriage. Life was coming together in ways I couldn't have possibly imagined, and for the first time, restorative sleep came naturally.

Along with my consulting and media appearances as an expert on crisis and reputation, I also wrote an occasional column for our local newspaper, the *Sag Harbor Express*.

Brigette, a mom from our children's school, suggested I write my next column about how to get happy when dealing with stress. I named the article, "One Less, One More – The Sag Harbor Effect."

The words flowed. My article suggested that every day, both individually and as a community, we systematically do less of what's not working and doesn't feel good, and instead, choose to follow our hearts and do more of what we know feels good, so that together we create profound peace, happiness, harmony and success.

Within hours of the column running, "One Less, One More" went viral. Soon, I was receiving the same request from all over the world: "Please, write a book."

And, so I did.

Yes, my father abandoned our family and left us near penniless. Yes, I was homeless at seventeen, flunked out of high school, and don't hold a college degree. I overcame an eleven-year drug addiction, a failed marriage, lost my home in a fire, and faced near financial collapse several times. But you know what? I consider myself the luckiest guy on the planet, and I remain eternally grateful for my magnificent life.

Every day – every moment – affords me the luxury of following my heart. I am happily married to my best friend, and we have two wonderful, independent and healthy children. I have countless friends and an extraordinary extended family. I have experienced unimaginable success in every aspect of my life. I consider myself blessed.

Believe me, if I can rise above life's problems and live with abundance, accomplishment, good health, joy, love and prosperity, so can you.

So, let's give it a go.

One Less. One More.

# One

## One Less. One More.

*An unexamined life*
*is not worth living.*
*– Socrates*

**There is a collective awakening** across the planet, a realization, really, that all of us are part of something much bigger than our individual lives. You are so much more than the labels of your name, body, family, religion, job, financial position, geography, or nationality.

As one of more than seven billion people on the planet, and intricately connected to the greater whole, your heart is opening to the possibility that you are far more powerful than you've previously understood. Today, right now, you have the inherent ability to consciously create an extraordinarily happy and fulfilling life that, through heart-directed intentions and beliefs, can boldly benefit all of humanity.

Heaven is not out there, somewhere mysteriously in the ether, but really, in here, deep within your soul, right now, and present at all times. Your life is not a task or chore, but the endless discovery and expression of your true and essential nature.

Your natural condition is to be free, happy, in love, healthy, joyful, prosperous, abundant, radiant and enthusiastic, and your life's purpose is to experience and express your truth, who you truly are. You are here for a purpose, and never alone. Your thoughts, emotions, and actions have vast consequences, and on more levels than you can possibly imagine, you intentionally create your life.

Regardless of your religion, social status, occupation, geography, gender or race, you, like billions of other human beings around the world, feel a growing discontent and concern for your physical, mental, emotional and spiritual well-being. And, like so many others, you recognize that our current culture's lifestyle is no longer acceptable.

Up until now, we've been taught to attack what we fear, champion only the glow of youth, and dismiss the gift of age, maturity and wisdom. Civility has been replaced with an ugly acceptance of greed, rage, vulgarity and contempt.

We have unconsciously believed that to be right, someone else must be wrong, and that it is perfectly acceptable to fight, hurt or kill other human beings in order to defend and protect our righteous position.

For over a century we've allowed ourselves to be manipulated into believing consumption is the key to happiness. The financial markets, along with retail and movie sales, are reported with urgency and inflated importance, while media news coverage is now mostly delivered as biased opinion, not objective information.

We eat excessive portions of fake, fatty, unhealthy modified foods, while voraciously drinking highly sweetened chemicals. Many continue smoking, while others pollute their bodies with drug and alcohol abuse.

Through our senses, we consume violence, horror, racism, perverted misogynistic sex, criminal glorification, gossip, reputational assassinations, constant criticism and nasty, denigrating prejudices, often masquerading as humor. And although mental health experts tell us once we witness a violent or horrific act, whether real or simulated, we can never – ever – erase that imagery from our minds; we still allow ourselves and our children to become desensitized to shock, horror and cruelty, creating a callous cynicism that blocks true joy and beauty.

Further, we're taught by many to believe actions against nature have little to no consequences, that there is an unlimited supply of natural resources, such as air, land and water, and that we are alone and separate from each other, both here on Earth and throughout the universe.

We're also told life is a random act of chance, and while some win, most don't. And worst of all, we've allowed ourselves to become victims of fear, hate, shame, jealousy, prejudice, guilt and anger.

We've permitted ourselves to become addicted and manipulated; standing witness to multiple daily horrors, knowing deep in our soul we, as a culture, are being poisoned and controlled.

Yet, as true addicts, we turn back for more.

None of this, on any level, feels good.

Although these belief systems contribute to addictions, wars, domestic violence, divorce, criminal activity and disease, the good news is the resulting despair and unhappiness is also fueling a collective awareness – an awakening – that there is an alternative, an option to this madness, including the pursuit of love, happiness, freedom, compassion, peace, joy, harmony, forgiveness, gratitude, service, enthusiasm, passion and unity, all conscious choices that result in feeling good.

Just as the universe continues expanding and is never complete, the same is true for your life's path. You are pure energy, and like all energy, your essence can neither be created nor destroyed. Your life is part of a continuing cycle, and while here on Earth, you have the moment-to-moment ability to dramatically change your life for the better.

Yet, as you become conscious and aware of the very real possibility of experiencing and expressing a life fulfilled, you now face an even greater challenge, as you ask yourself: What *do* I want? What *is* my purpose? Who *am* I? What *do* I do now? How can I change my life? How can I find true happiness?

Good on ya, mate, as my Australian friends say. These questions awaken your heart's calling, your personal exploration deep into the depth of your soul, and the joyful revelation of why you were born.

Throughout history, saints, avatars, leaders and everyday people alike, found themselves asking these same questions as they, too, began awakening to their life's purpose.

What these daring souls learned, as you will, too, is that there are just a few simple and profound steps to self-realization, change, happiness and personal mastery.

## One Less. One More.

The first step to happiness and personal mastery is to start now. Not later, tomorrow, next year, after school, or when you feel better. Start now.

Next, you must make a conscious decision to follow your heart, be happy and change your life. These are the most important decisions of your entire life, and require some form of a daily reminder.

Next, on a daily basis, you must choose from your present life one less negative, resistant, or bad feeling, thought or action, and let it go.

Call this, One Less.

Further, also on a daily basis, you must listen to your heart's calling and choose one more positive or good feeling, thought or action, and embrace it.

Call this, One More.

One Less. One More.

Take time each and every day to celebrate your progress, your life's journey, and consciously choose to repeat the One Less, One More process again tomorrow.

That's it.

Do the math. One Less, One More is an ageless formula that when practiced slowly, steadily and perpetually, results in unimaginable, incremental, sustainable success, change, and happiness.

One Less, One More is a life-long journey – not a destination – one glorious day after the next.

Substantial change is a process and takes time. A lot of time. And, as all masters know, true mastery requires a lifetime of practice.

One reason so many of us often fail at major transformation is because we try too much, too quickly. Life altering change is an evolutionary process, and if changes are forced or pressured to materialize outside of a natural cycle, the entire system will resist and, ultimately, fail.

Imagine planting an acorn today that produces a giant oak tree tomorrow. Or discovering you have a good singing voice, and within a few hours are performing at New York City's Madison Square Garden. Or meeting someone you think is cute, and by nightfall you're married with three children. Your head always wants to speed things up, but your heart needs to savor each moment and slow things down.

What matters is that today, and every day, you make a conscious decision to follow your heart, be happy and deliberately change your life. Then, right now, intentionally let go of one negative, resistant element from your life that doesn't feel good, and conversely, choose to experience one more positive thing that feels great. That's it.

I use One Less, One More to be a better parent, spouse, lover, friend, citizen of the planet, advisor, organic gardener, writer, photographer, cook, clammer and traveler.

For example, I now use less chemicals in my garden and

more organic fertilizer. I shop less in the big supermarkets and more at local farmers' markets. I worry less what people think about me, and instead consider more ways I can contribute to humanity.

I spend less time worrying if I'm going to catch any clams, and more time enjoying being out in the sun surrounded by warm water. I walk less with my head down and more looking up at the world around me. I focus less on my fear of death, and more on being in the present moment and alive today.

I frown less and smile more. I play the role of father and husband less, instead, contributing more as an active, engaged, family participant. I look for fewer reasons to be upset, and more reasons to be grateful.

I make less risky investments, and conversely, invest more in companies involved in corporate citizenry. Now when I travel, I consciously pack less and walk more. And in my role as an advisor, I make a point of talking less and listening more.

The list for how I use One Less, One More is endless, because every day presents unlimited opportunities to do *less* of what doesn't feel good, and *more* of what aligns to my heart's purpose, which feels great.

From a transcendent perspective, several family members, friends and clients use One Less, One More to be more "faith-based" Christians, Catholics and Muslims; others use One Less, One More to be more observant Jews; several clients use One Less, One More to explore their spirituality; several people use One Less, One More to improve their Zen meditation and yoga practice, and a friend of over thirty years, an atheist, who doesn't believe in God at all, uses One Less, One More to "just live a better life."

Practicing One Less, One More requires no special training or skills. It's not important to have a picture formed in your mind of the future, or what you want to achieve, or even how or why you arrived here in your present life. That will come.

You only need to believe you were born to be happy, and that by practicing the math of One Less, One More, over time, your life will fundamentally and beneficially transform.

Try it. By consciously letting go of some form of daily negativity, and conversely, embracing something positive and heart-felt every day, your life will change as you become happy, move toward life mastery, and successfully fulfill your heart's dreams, goals and desires.

So, together, let's take this journey to follow our hearts, be happy and change slowly.

One Less. One More.

# Two

## Follow Your Heart

**Less:** Feeling Bad
**More:** Feeling Good

> *To know one thing,*
> *you must know the opposite.*
> *– Henry Moore*

**Out of more than one hundred billion people** since the beginning of time, and the countless others to follow, you are a singularly unique and remarkable human being.

Your birth alone is a miracle. From conception, you faced extraordinary obstacles just getting here, and through events still mostly a mystery to modern humankind, emerged a living, breathing, human being. You are an amazing aspect of this universe, indescribably special, and inexhaustible in original possibilities. You materialized from eternal, infinite space, into something so unique that for the rest of eternity, no one will ever remotely resemble you.

No one has, or ever will, be able to experience or

express your singular point of view, which is why it is so important, both for you and all humanity, that you follow your heart.

You may not have a clue what your heart desires, yet rest assured, you were born for a magnificent purpose, and when on a daily basis you consciously choose less of what doesn't feel good, and more of what does, you are headed in the right direction.

In this very moment, right now as you read this, you are aware of many things in your life that don't feel good, aspects of your existence that no longer work, and you want less of them.

Conversely, you know, or more accurately, experience, a burning desire deep within you to change your life, be happy and do more fulfilling things that feel good.

Once you know what doesn't feel good, and consciously choose less of it, and grow in your awareness of what does feel good, and choose more of that, you are on an unstoppable path to extraordinary success, happiness, health, wealth, and internal peace.

This is One Less, One More.

## Your Purpose

You were born to follow your heart and be happy.

It's really that simple.

Regardless of your current belief system, you, in this life, are on an astonishing journey to discover and fulfill your dreams and desires.

Listen. Your heart is calling you to an adventure, a

lifelong exploration of your true self, and the revelation of your life's purpose. If you listen, truly listen, each and every moment is calling you to follow your heart and be happy. And once you acknowledge your heart's calling, nothing will ever be the same.

What you are hearing is not some vague voice from your head taunting you with a hazy promise of a potentially better life sometime in the future. Instead, you are witnessing your heart's awakening, the opening and expansion of your consciousness, and the very real fulfillment of your goals, dreams and desires.

Your life's purpose, which you began experiencing even before you were born, is to feel good and follow your heart. On this leg of your endless journey, you are traveling in an extraordinary vehicle called the human body, a structure so complex it requires over one hundred *trillion* living cells to function properly. Although, to enjoy the ride you are not obliged to understand the intricate functioning of your body, you may still be interested in noting that from the largest organ to the tinniest quantum particle, your physical body is a complete and evolved biological feedback system specifically designed to assist you on your journey.

The sole function of your physical existence, from a follicle of hair, to a singular, remarkable T cell, is to provide you in any moment, and on myriad levels, with specific feedback on whether or not you are aligned to your heart's purpose.

Your body is the most elaborate machine on the planet,

yet uniquely customized for self-discovery, expression and creation. Your body's exclusive purpose is serving you on this life's journey as you discover and fulfill your heart's desires.

Every cell in your body is a living organism which creates energy, reproduces, and contains universal consciousness and intelligence. Every level of your existence, every aspect of your being, every piece of your substance, both seen and invisible, is unique and simultaneously connects you to every other function and system throughout the entire universe. You are both a magnet and a beacon for the discovery, expression and fulfillment of your heart's desires.

*You are both a magnet and a beacon for the discovery, expression, and fulfillment of your heart's desires.*

Your physical body contains many individual systems, including an immune, circulatory, nervous, reproductive, digestive, skeletal, respiratory and muscular system, all operating independently and without any direct conscious input from you. You don't even have to think to keep yourself alive. Without any conscious thought, your heart beats, you breathe, sleep, digest food and keep your eyes clean by blinking. Further, your senses provide a spectacular array of perceptions, allowing you to constantly readjust your life's experience based on what feels good, or more precisely, what does and doesn't serve your heart's purpose.

## In and Out

Like one complete breath or an ocean wave, there are two distinct, yet connected aspects to following your heart.

The first part to following your heart is self-discovery, the inward movement. You were born to discover, to remember, who you are. Every human being shares this adventure, yet miraculously, there are no two similar paths. You are an extraordinary, whole, connected, complete being, meant to feel good now.

The outward movement, the second part to following your heart, is consciously acknowledging that simply by living your life you are a creator, the universe's storyteller. Every aspect of your being, including your birth, body, point of view, the decisions and choices you make, your relationships, what you create (or destroy), and ultimately, what you leave behind, are unique and remarkable expressions of who you are. Whether you are conscious of the process or not, *every* choice you make changes the world.

## Follow Your Heart

Following your heart is an extraordinary journey that started long before you were born and will continue long after you discard this shell, your body.

Allow your belief system to expand just enough to consider that as the universe is unfathomable and infinite, so is your heart's journey. Like a runner in a relay race, consciously choosing to follow your heart is a decision to enter a race already started. Grabbing the baton, you continue to run until you hand it over to the next runner, who will also be you, just in a different form. Following your heart is a voyage, not a destination.

Further, your life's story is packed with astonishing circumstances, a unique point of view, a lifetime of deep and powerful emotions, the interaction with surprisingly complex and unique characters, countless obstacles, the path to great heights and remarkable lows, all while discovering personal and universal truths about yourself. Through a lifetime of expression and creation, your life is a symbol, a metaphor, a pointer to humanity's collective journey, told in an entirely new and meaningful way.

You are here for a reason so unique that the only way to express your heart's purpose is by living your life to its full potential.

You were born to expand, create and explore, not contract, fear or live in lack. In the past, you may have felt silly, afraid or uncomfortable acknowledging that you were being called to a special adventure. Yet intuitively, you know that now – right now – is the time to change your life, follow your heart and be happy.

I live close to the ocean on the eastern end of New York's Long Island, and not long ago, I was on the beach with my family and a man walked up to me and asked, "Are you the guy who moved out here from New York City?"

I smiled, answering, "Yes."

"Yeah, my wife told me about you," he replied. "I just wish I could move out here, too; but I can't."

"Why?" I asked him.

"I'm a dentist with a big practice in the city and I can't just walk away."

I told him my job was helping people reach their goals by following their hearts, and that I've counseled many folks who successfully moved their professional service practices from one location to another. I even offered him several viable ideas to consider, and asked him what he really wanted in his heart-of-hearts.

"That's what scares me," he said, "I really don't know *what* I want."

"That's normal," I said, reassuringly. "Don't worry now about what you do want, tell me what you don't want."

"I know I don't want to be a dentist," he said, sadly. "I know I don't want to live in the city. And I know I don't want to keep chasing money at the expense of my children or marriage, but I made my bed, and now I have to sleep in it."

"That's not true," I told him. "You just made the wrong bed."

He laughed, and asked what to do.

I told him to consider that today is the absolute perfect place to start his new life, and that without making large, wholesale, disruptive changes, he can begin everyday by acknowledging one less thing that doesn't feel good and letting it go, and also finding things that feel great, and embracing at least one more of those every day.

"That I can do," he said, as we discussed a few of his options.

We kept in touch and today, although still a dentist in

the city, he's taken on a couple of partners to reduce his level of responsibility, bought a home in the Connecticut woods, travels the world volunteering his time and dental skills with an international health care organization, and is slowly transitioning himself and his family for a move out of the city.

Shifting his life will take time. Yet by slowly and intentionally eliminating what's not working, and moving in the direction of following his heart, the dentist doesn't have to start from scratch and throw out his entire life wholesale, which, unfortunately, so many people do when stuck in an all-or-nothing approach to their lives.

Writing in an email, he said, "Knowing that every day all I have to do is find one thing that doesn't feel good, and do less of it, and choose one thing that feels good, and do more of it, changed my life forever." And, more important, Dr. Dentist feels great, his marriage is on track, and he is now consciously pursuing his passions and following his heart.

What are you hearing in your head right now?

If you're like many of my clients, you're experiencing "The Boat," that sound of "but, but, but, but, but . . ."

"But, the dentist has more money than me."

"But, he's a dentist, I'm only a student."

"But, that dentist works in the city, I'm in a small town."

"But, how can I earn a living/support my family/go to college if I follow my dreams?"

"But, my circumstance is different, because . . ."

"But, you don't know the terrible things I did in my past."

"But, I've never been happy."

"But, who would ever accept me as an actor/coach/ dancer/police officer/scientist/accountant/body builder/ gardener/human rights activist/baker/veterinarian/ marine biologist/entrepreneur?"

"But, what if I fail?"

But, but, but.

Stop. Take a deep breath. And know, from right here, where you are in this very moment is the perfect place to start following your heart.

There is a sense of enormity burning through you that won't allow you to settle anymore, which is why you are here. You are awakening to your connection to the universe, the possibility of your own vastness; with an ever deeper knowing that what you are feeling is absolutely achievable.

From deep within you is this longing to emerge from this cave of shadows, your home of the ordinary, where you've been living by everyone else's rules. No more. This is your awakening, your authentic journey toward mastering your life.

And don't worry if you can't always hear your heart's calling. That's perfectly normal. What's more important now is that you start becoming aware of what doesn't feel good, and do less of it. And conversely, start discovering everything that feels good, and do more of it. Clear the leaves and the lawn will appear.

Few people truly know what they want from their lives today, let alone in one, two, or ten years down the road. Yet they, like you, are certain of one thing: they know exactly what no longer feels good, and what no longer fits in their lives.

Regardless of what you perceive as your limitations, you can, from right here, consciously choose to follow your heart, be happy and slowly change your life.

No "ifs," "ands" or "buts" about it.

Simply say, "I choose to follow my heart and be happy."

And with that, the journey begins.

# Choice

In every moment you have only one choice: Do you consciously choose to follow your heart, feel good, live the life you were born to live, or not?

There is no right or wrong, it's all simply whether, in any moment, you are aligned to fulfilling your life's purpose or not.

Even if you never answered your heart's calling, or don't know what you dream or desire from your life, it's *perfectly* okay, because now, at the very least, you are becoming aware of what feels good and what doesn't, which is the awakening of your soul.

You know when you feel sad, depressed, lonely, angry, jealous and guilty. And, you know when you feel happy, orgasmic, delighted, loving, compassionate and kind.

When you feel good, it means you are aligned to your life's purpose, and, if you so choose, you can continue feeling even better.

When you don't feel good, it simply means you are not aligned to your greater purpose, and, if you so choose, can learn and grow from the situation and switch to feeling good. If, however, you consciously choose to continue feeling bad, then you can also use that information for feedback, and the moment you choose to return to your heart's path, you will instantly feel good again.

Essentially, you either choose to feel good or not. If your choice is to feel good, then you're moving in the direction of continuing to feel good. Conversely, it's nearly impossible to feel good when you choose to feel bad.

Feeling good or bad is a conscious decision. And even if you currently believe feelings just happen to you, at least consider that, once you become aware of your feelings, the choice to continue feeling good or bad is a conscious decision on your part.

Remember, in every conscious moment you have only one choice: Do you choose to feel good, or not? Do you, regardless of the external situation, choose to be present and live from your heart, looking for reasons to feel good, or do you resist the present moment and look for reasons to feel bad?

Your life, and every moment in your life, is a choice.

You have the choice in every moment to either feel good, or not.

You have the choice in every moment to either align with your life's purpose, or not.

And even if you don't know your life's purpose, you have the choice in every moment to either seek your life's purpose, or not.

You have the choice in every moment to believe in your

heart's calling, or not.

You have the choice in every moment to live in fear, or with faith and courage.

You have the choice to make this moment either better, or worse.

You have the choice to either try and control every moment, or simply let go.

You have the choice in every moment to either follow your heart, or the ego.

You have the choice in every moment to either express truth, or not.

You have the choice in every moment to either resist or yield.

You have the choice in every moment to start fresh, or continue repeating behaviors.

You have the choice in every moment to either become accountable, or blame someone or something else.

You have the choice in every moment to forgive yourself and others, or not.

And in every moment you have the choice to live life by chance, or choice.

It doesn't matter whether you are walking the dog, cleaning a toilet, making love, building a business, camping, recuperating from an illness, sewing a button, or taking a test. Are you choosing to feel good, or are you resisting this moment and feeling bad?

Look at it this way. Where you are at this moment is, well, where you are. You can't go backwards, can't change anything from the past, and although you might like to try, you can't change the people around you. You really have only one of two options right now. Do you choose to resist the present moment and feel bad, or do you come present, let go of everything outside of your control, take a deep breath, and allow your heart's purpose to flow through you and feel good?

Happiness is *always* your choice.

# Resisting and Allowing

Not feeling good on any level, whether physical, mental, emotional, or spiritual, is some form of resistance to your heart's purpose, and is the *One Less* part of One Less, One More.

Aspects of resisting your heart's purpose include fear, doubt, worry, judgment, prejudice, competition, having to be right, control, anger, blame, entitlement and aggression. Resisting your heart's purpose *never* feels good.

Experiencing resistance to your heart's calling is neither good nor bad.

Resistance is simply part of a remarkable and very personal feedback system which keeps you aligned to your greater purpose. When you feel good, you're on the right path. When you don't feel good, you are out of alignment and in some way, off purpose.

Resisting your heart's purpose is like holding your breath; it goes against your own survival. When you resist your purpose, you literally cut yourself off from your life force, and eventually every aspect of your entire life experiences distress (dis-stress) or disease (dis-ease). All forms of resistance work against fulfilling your heart's purpose, because you're ultimately working against your own true nature.

Although feeling good always feels better than feeling bad, feeling bad is just an indicator, a well-honed gauge, a pointer, telling you that in some way, on some level, whether aware of it or not, you are out of alignment to your heart's purpose.

When your car's gas gauge points to empty, it's informing you that your vehicle will soon require more gas if you wish to proceed. You can certainly choose to feel bad about an empty gas tank, but regardless of how you feel, if you want to keep moving down the road, you need to fill your tank with more gas.

When you resist fulfilling your dreams and desires, and don't consciously change the way you feel, you work against the very reason you were born. Considering how often you resist feeling good by choosing to feel bad, sounds a bit like insanity.

Conversely, allowing yourself the pleasure of experiencing your heart's dreams and desires is the *One More* aspect of One Less, One More.

Consciously choosing to be happy and following your heart, allowing your life's purpose to flow through you, creates the space, openness and opportunity to understand your true nature, and, ultimately, experience love, happiness, bliss, beauty, peace, harmony and success. When you allow your heart's desires to flow through you, you step off into the river of life, and instead of struggling upstream, you allow the river's current to effortlessly take you downstream. When you allow yourself to follow your heart, life becomes exciting, abundant and fun.

Consciously choosing to connect with your heart's purpose includes the experience of courage, improved health, passion, faith, unity, inspiration, creativity, compassion, flexibility, appreciation, service, generosity and enthusiasm. Allowing yourself the pure pleasure and excitement of following your heart *always* feels good.

Resisting your heart's purpose feels bad, disconnected, off-purpose and lonely.

When aligned to your heart's dreams and desires, you are allowing your life's purpose to flow smoothly, and you feel good. When you are out of alignment to your life's purpose, you are resisting your heart's calling, and you feel bad.

# Losing Katy

Our small village lost a beautiful twelve-year-old girl, Katy, to a rare form of liver cancer. Our family and community were devastated, and although we all pulled together for two years to support Katy and her family, she lost her battle the week between Christmas and New Year's Day.

Clare,* a local parent and friend, called to say that losing Katy had thrown her into a terrible funk.

I asked Clare to describe her "funk."

"Losing this beautiful child has brought up a lot of feelings," Clare confided. "I'm feeling bad for Katy's family.

I'm worried about my own children.

"Katy shouldn't have died so young. Sometimes, I can't believe we all die. I worry how this is going to affect my children and Katy's friends, and if they're going to be scarred for life. And I just feel sad that Katy had to suffer."

I asked my friend to choose just one of her bad feelings.

"Okay, maybe selfishly I worry the most about losing my own children."

I suggested instead of labeling her fear of losing her own children as "bad," or "selfish," that she consider her feelings as feedback for being out of alignment with her true heart's calling during this time of loss.

I asked Clare to focus for a moment on how it felt thinking about the possibility of losing her children.

"Losing my kids is my single worst fear," Clare said, with a slight tremble in her voice. "Just thinking about it makes me sick."

I suggested Clare consciously acknowledge those "sickening" thoughts as feedback for being out of alignment with her heart's purpose, and that, just for today, she choose to mentally release those scary thoughts. Instead, I told Clare to pivot her mind to images of her children very much alive, active, healthy and happy, anything she could think of that would bring her instant and immeasurable joy.

Clare's voice got stronger as she told me, "I feel so blessed God allowed me these angels, and I am grateful every day for their smiles, laughter, and even all their problems. I was born to be these children's mother, and I just love them so."

With almost no effort, Clare shifted her energy from worry to gratitude, from fear in her head, to joy in her heart.

I ran into Clare a few days later, and she was happy and bubbly.

"I'm still sad about losing Katy," she said, "but I don't feel gloomy or afraid anymore. Knowing my fears are just feedback to keep me connected to my own life's purpose allowed me to see Katy's passing as a reminder of the sanctity of life, the gift of living in Sag Harbor, how lucky we were to have spent time with her, and that each day as a mother is a blessing beyond words."

## Your Life is An Adventure – Start Now!

Here's something I want you to consider:

You chose the exact life you're in right now. Everything in this moment is perfect as a starting place to pivot into the direction of following your heart. Even before you were born, you've been moving in a very precise direction for a very specific purpose.

And, unless you believe your birth and everything else in your life – including reading this book at this very moment – is a fluke, a random act of nature, then you must accept that your life has a very specific purpose. And that purpose, your life's purpose, is very simply to follow your heart and be happy.

As a child, you had abundant longings, yearnings and desires, and, if you're honest with yourself, you've always felt you were born for a higher purpose. But what?

Maybe you've always wanted to ride horses, write

a book, live in another country, become a doctor, start a homeless shelter, become a scientist, be physically fit, raise chickens, travel, grow things, jump from a plane, explore, expand, inspire. Every person on the planet, including and especially you, is a seed of unlimited possibilities.

In my case, since I was a child, from my earliest conscious memories, all I've ever wanted to be is a storyteller. My life's purpose, my heart's desire, my call to adventure, is finding new and exciting ways to tell heart-centered stories that positively change the world.

I've also spent a great deal of time discovering new ways to feel good and follow my heart, including spending abundant time with my family, learning to fly, training in karate, clamming, writing movies that I can also act in, driving motorcycles, and discovering small, family-run, tucked-away restaurants and dive bars across the globe. Over time, these are some of my *One Mores* that feel wonderful and help connect me to my life's purpose.

Conversely, I'm also aware of the many things that don't connect with my heart's purpose.

For example, to this day, I can't imagine working for someone else. I've never wanted to be a doctor, lawyer or politician. I have no talent for drawing, don't enjoy swimming or being cold, and have no interest in living anywhere far from an ocean (except for Paris!). I've never enjoyed beets, single malt scotch or ratatouille. I can't stand still for very long, never been good at math, haven't been able to form an emotional connection to opera, and I much prefer playing sports to watching it.

There is nothing wrong or lacking in what I like or don't, it's just that in this life, on my current path, there are certain aspects of experience that align or don't with my current life's purpose. And as I change, my likes and dislikes change, too.

As I'm sure your parents told you, you came into this world with preferences, talents, hopes, dreams and desires, demonstrating that you were already connected to the life you came here to create.

My son, Connor, and I went shopping at a large music store with every kind of musical instrument imaginable. Stopping by the percussion department, a three-year-old boy was playing the drums. He wasn't banging on the drums; he was making music, creating a beat. This toddler wouldn't stop playing until a salesman moved him along. His parents, who were with him, said, "His whole world is drumming. Ever since he was two, all he wants to do is drum."

It was so clear: this boy was born to play drums. Your skills and talents may not be as obvious, or maybe your life's calling was clearer a long time ago, before you got so good at burying your feelings. It doesn't matter.

You were born whole and complete, entering this world with an extraordinary and unique purpose. The dreams and desires you experience – your heart's calling – came as the potential of what you were born to achieve. Your heart, soul, mind and body, along with the entire universe, serve one purpose: supporting you to be happy and follow your heart.

## Life Mastery

You are the master and creator of your life. And whether you understand, accept or believe this to be true, it changes nothing and makes no difference to the universe.

You either choose to acknowledge your heart's desires and allow *more* of those experiences into and through your life, resulting in joy, harmony, love and so many more good feelings, or you choose to resist and ignore your heart's purpose, experiences and expressions, resulting in a life out of alignment, filled with sadness, anger, resentment, depression, dis-ease, fear, hatred, greed, jealousy and more.

Whether you allow or resist your life's purpose, it still comes down to you creating your life, and having the choice in every moment to either fulfill more of your heart's desires, or not.

First Lady Michelle Obama said at a round table meeting on February 10, 2009, three weeks after her husband, Barack, won the first term of his presidency, "There is no magic dust that was sprinkled on my head or on Barack's head. We . . . figured out one day that our fate was in our own hands."

What does your heart desire? And why do you desire it?

When you experience and fulfill your heart's desires, you are also expanding the universe through the amazing act of creation. The unlimited and eternal universe is available to you in each and every moment because without you, there would be no universe. Without you, and every other human being, there would be no expressed art, sport, teaching, learning, passion or enlightenment.

You were born to experience your heart's desires. And what's even more extraordinary is that no one has, or ever will, share your unique vision, point of view or unique truth. No one, ever.

Your life is a story of epic proportions, and you are the storyteller creating the plot, theme, tone, characters, each chapter, and every scene exactly as you wish. What happens to you is irrelevant; it's what you do with what happens to you that makes the difference.

Right now, as you read this, you can feel an excitement and a tension pulling you in one of two ways. One feeling comes from the tug of resistance, that feeling of fear, disbelief or disdain.

Resistance screams from inside your head: "I can't be wealthy, pain-free, happy, lose weight, live in the home of my dreams, stop smoking, start a new business, or find true love."

However, if you choose to feel good, and allow your heart to express itself, you can feel the excitement and expectation of the possibilities, as you confidently hear, "Yes, I can be happy and create my future!"

*Great spirits have always found violent opposition from mediocrities. The latter cannot understand it when a man does not thoughtlessly submit to hereditary prejudices, but honestly and courageously uses his intelligence and fulfills the duty to express the results of his thought in clear form.*

*– Albert Einstein*

I don't need to guess what you're thinking, because over the last twenty-five years, I've counseled hundreds of successful people all over the world who, just like you, when awakening to their heart's calling, say the same thing: "Just because I desire it doesn't mean I can have it. That's just selfish."

Says who? Your parents? Teachers? Religious leaders? Well-meaning friends? The voice in your head?

Anyone who tells you that you cannot, should not, better not, follow your heart, be happy and change your life, is wrong. Although well-meaning, those negative and mistaken suggestions are precisely the *One Less* resistant thoughts you're going to remove from your life, one day at a time. Think of the insanity in discovering your life's purpose – your heart's passions and desires – and then consciously *choosing* to resist it, moving, instead, in the opposite direction.

I've worked with countless leaders and celebrities who question their heart's path because they've already achieved so much in the way of influence, money, accomplishment and prestige, that they feel guilty wanting more.

And yet, when I ask these successful people if they've yet fulfilled their heart's desires, they *always* say, "No." Although many are famous, wealthy and powerful, they still have so much more to do, especially when they awaken to following their heart. Some want to go on and feed the hungry; others are called to spend more time with their children; many want to build another sustainable business, while some want to spend a month in an

Indian ashram, play a musical instrument, or learn to do something lighthearted – like one successful middle-aged, single woman who, after making millions of dollars, chose to become a professional clown.

*The world changes when you consciously choose to follow your heart. The question then becomes, "Are my actions making the world better or worse?"*

Once someone starts awakening to feeling happy and following their heart, I'll hear hypothetical questions like, "What if killing makes me feel good?" (Many male leaders like to hunt, and often ask this question.)

Consider this: When you hunt, make sure you take the time to see how it feels deep inside. If you feel an internal urging not to kill, or, like many cultures, to bless your prey before you take a life, or to enjoy hunting in nature without killing, simply follow your heart.

Another popular question: "What if bacon makes me feel good?"

Your body will give you the answer. (Personally, I believe bacon makes everything better.)

Or another hypothetical question I once heard is, "What if having sex with multiple strangers without my husband knowing makes me feel good?"

If you're truly following your heart, the universe will provide that answer very quickly.

Your life's purpose is unique, and only you know in your heart-of-hearts what path is aligned with your life's purpose. I'm not a psychologist, judge, moralist, scientist, doctor or guru. I'm just a guy who, over the years as a crisis expert, discovered that people who consistently choose to change their lives for the better, align with their life's purpose, and follow their heart, end up happier, healthier, more fulfilled and accomplished.

One Less, One More is just one formula for achieving happiness, a path to help raise your consciousness about making choices – consistent, conscious, incremental, choices. Some of your choices may be compassionate, others may be neutral, and others may be selfish and/or illegal. Observe your intentions, follow your heart, and then choose.

There are always consequences to your choices, and that's all the path to life mastery requires you to consider: "What are my intentions? What am I feeling? What am I choosing? Am I aligned with my heart's purpose?"

Becoming conscious, asking questions, and looking for your heart's feedback is the beauty of the One Less, One More journey.

# Go For It

You are here because you are being called to a greater good, something more than you already have. And don't worry if you don't know now what that something "more" is, you will. You are stirred, restless, inspired and ready. You are listening to your unfettered soul calling you from the depth of your being.

Be kind to yourself, because as you understand what

you want, you will also become aware of what you don't want. It's all good.

The *One Less* parts of your adventure are what no longer fit in your life. This is so important to fulfilling your life's purpose, because until you remove those obstacles, obstructions and barriers, you can never align with your heart and move into your authentic, exciting future.

And the *One More* parts of your life are everything that contribute to you feeling happy, inspired and alive. It takes commitment and courage to follow your heart, but once you start down your true life's path, it won't make sense to ever turn back.

One Less, One More.

## Get Ready

What's important is that you allow yourself to hear your heart's calling. Take note of everything, and judge nothing. Be a screen door, letting the winds of this new awakening blow through you, and simply be conscious and aware.

You may want to carry a notepad, jotting down insights as they arise. Notice everything you resist or that just doesn't feel good. Become aware of what may now appear as coincidences, but, as you'll learn later, are just perfectly fitting moments that on some level you've created. Also, notice everything, both the big and small things that feel good, the connections to aligning with your internal feedback system.

**One Less. One More.**

*Your time is limited, so don't waste it living someone else's life. Don't be trapped by dogma – which is living with the results of other people's thinking. Don't let the noise of others' opinions drown out your own inner voice. And most important, have the courage to follow your heart and intuition. They somehow already know what you truly want to become. Everything else is secondary.*

*– Steve Jobs*

Take a deep breath. Come present. Listen to what you're hearing deep inside. Consciously choose less of what makes you feel bad, while also choosing more things that align with your heart's calling.

Because now, you've got to believe.

# One Less. One More.
# Steps

1. Start now.
2. Come present.
3. Consciously choose to follow your heart, be happy and change slowly.
4. Today, choose one less negative, resistant or bad feeling, thought or action, and let it go. One Less.
5. Today, choose one more positive or good feeling thought or action, and embrace it. One More.
6. Celebrate your progress.
7. Repeat tomorrow.

**One Less. One More.**

# Three

## Believe

**Less:** Fear
**More:** Awareness

> *"I can't believe that!" said Alice.*
> *"Can't you?" the Queen said in a pitying tone. "Try*
> *again: draw a long breath, and shut your eyes."*
> *Alice laughed. "There's no use trying," she said,*
> *"one can't believe impossible things."*
> *"I daresay you haven't had much practice," said the*
> *Queen. "When I was your age, I always did it for*
> *half an hour a day. Why sometimes I believed as*
> *many as six impossible things before breakfast!"*
> *– Lewis Carroll*, Alice's Adventures in Wonderland
> and Through the Looking Glass

**It's one thing to do something familiar**, to repeat a behavior, or return to a place you already know. But risking the decision to follow your heart, to consciously become a co-creator with the universe, and believe you were born to be happy, is the remarkable act of a courageous soul.

Initially, the prospect of change is often too scary for

mere mortals like you and me to handle. At first, you may think you're open to following your heart, finding a new job, quitting a bad habit, coming out, standing up for yourself, dealing with your anger, running for Congress, raising honey bees, starting a new relationship, becoming an entrepreneur, or moving out on your own. Yet, almost immediately, you experience fear and resistance to your plans.

Often, the opposition to following your heart is external. As you share your newfound enthusiasm with others, it's not long before well-intentioned doses of someone else's advice and counsel flushes the dangerous venom of fear, doubt and worry, through your veins.

Maybe you chose to follow your heart because you're bored and had enough of an unfulfilling existence. Or maybe you're at a place in your life where you feel unsettled and restless. Or, possibly, through a series of events resulting in a crisis, you make the leap to follow your heart, and find yourself thrust into a totally foreign situation.

Regardless, when the space opens for you to follow your heart, you will also experience the tension of resistance and fear.

At first, when you awaken to the possibilities of a world so exciting, fulfilling and promising that it seems almost unreal and unattainable, it's perfectly normal to initially turn away.

Be kind and gentle with yourself as you awaken to your life's purpose, because just like a wobbly newborn fawn, it will take some time before you can walk with the strength of your new convictions.

Now is probably not the best time to loudly and publicly proclaim your newly found intention to make a billion dollars, perform stand-up comedy at New York's Carnegie Hall, become president of the United States, or create the next Google.

Mastering your life and fulfilling your heart's purpose is not a race, it's an adventure. Pushing too hard, too quickly, creates the fear and resistance of an equal and opposite reaction, which, unless used to your advantage, will ultimately work against your decision to follow your heart. Don't force it, feel it.

Although you may be open to the possibilities – or as some naysayers may tell you, the impossibilities – of being happy and living life according to your heart's purpose, the initial prospect of following your heart can feel terrifying, and for some, paralyzing.

*Believing you were born to be happy, feel good, experience your true nature, and use your life as an instrument of co-creation with the universe, is not something most of us are taught in childhood.*

## Barry Manilow

Fear sometimes gets the best of us, including me.

On a cold winter night toward the end of 1972, I attended Bette Midler's *The Divine Miss M* concert at Philadelphia's fabled Academy of Music. That night, Ms. Midler introduced her new musical director, a young Barry Manilow.

## One Less. One More.

Just before taking her intermission break, Ms. Midler, in her famous raspy voice, told the audience, "You're going to be hearing a lot more from this talented twenty-nine-year-old genius," and left the stage to Mr. Manilow as he began playing songs from his upcoming first album, *Barry Manilow I.*

Performing during Ms. Midler's intermission, Mr. Manilow seemed oblivious to the audience as they chatted, moved around, and left their seats to get snacks. Most everyone ignored him as he played, until something happened I've only ever seen in the movies.

Mr. Manilow began playing the last song in his set, "Could It Be Magic," which begins and ends with an excerpt from Chopin's Prelude in C-Minor, op. 28, no. 20.

As if Mr. Manilow were creating gravity, his music began to pull the audience in. A riveting performance, all the activity outside the main hall stopped, and the audience returned to their seats, spellbound. Even the ushers and souvenir vendors were drawn back into the concert hall. Mr. Manilow finished, and after the audience responded with a stunned moment of silence, everyone erupted into a standing ovation.

The next day I called Miles Lourie, Mr. Manilow's manager in New York, introducing myself as both a fan and a cub reporter for the Philadelphia suburban newspaper, the *Bucks County Courier Times*. I wanted an interview.

"Tell you what, kid," Mr. Lourie said, "Barry's in the studio right now finishing his first album, and I'll have him call you when he takes a break!"

When Mr. Manilow called a few hours later, my voice was shaking.

"Calm down," Mr. Manilow said. "I'm so happy you called, and Miles told me how much you dig my music."

I instantly relaxed and interviewed Mr. Manilow for almost an hour.

"Look," Mr. Manilow said, "I have to get back into the studio. But my friend [the singer] Melissa Manchester and I are having a small party in Manhattan this Saturday night, and [the comedian] Robert Klein will be there, and I would really like for you to come, too. Please join us. Ciao."

Excited, I ran around my apartment, calling friends, screaming at the top of my lungs. Not only did I get an interview with someone who I knew would soon be a major star, but I was invited to a New York City party!

I couldn't believe this was happening to me. All of my dreams were coming true: I was a working photojournalist, interviewing fascinating people, and now being invited to fun parties with famous people in New York City.

But then I got an attack of fear and the "what ifs . . ."

*What if I get there and Barry doesn't remember me?*

I called Miles Lourie back and made sure Mr. Manilow's invitation to the party was sincere.

"You bet," Mr. Lourie said. "He really likes your vibe, kid, and wants to meet you."

That wasn't enough. *What if something bad happens to me in New York City? What if no one likes me? What am I going to wear? Should I bring my camera? But if I don't get any photos, the newspaper won't pay for my trip, and I can't afford this on my own?*

For the entire week prior to the party, I sabotaged my joy. On Saturday morning, the day of the party, I was so overcome with dread; I stayed in bed for almost the whole day. I never found the courage to attend Barry Manilow's party.

To this day, I remain a Barry Manilow fan, and thank him for giving me my first big break. More important, though, is Mr. Manilow providing me with one of the universe's most powerful lessons: Never, ever, allow fear to be anything but feedback along your life's journey.

*Never, ever, allow fear to be anything but feedback along your life's journey.*

## Fear as Feedback

Welcome fear.

Remember this: Fear is good, because just as darkness makes the absence of light obvious, fear is immediate feedback for being out of alignment with your heart's intentions and life's purpose.

Imagine, for example, one of your lifelong dreams is driving cross-country.

Starting at the Santa Monica Pier on the Pacific Ocean in Los Angeles, you head east on Interstate 10 toward New York City. Proceeding along the highway, all the road signs point you in the right direction, which feels good because you're on course. You continue on for 1,700 miles, and all is well.

Around Des Moines, Iowa, you hear of a good barbecue restaurant and pull off Interstate 80 for dinner. After your meal, you get back in your car and, now dark and foggy, you head back on to the highway. But wait. Something's wrong. The road signs are now pointing north to Minneapolis – St. Paul, Minnesota, the Twin Cities – not east, the direction you want to be headed.

Des Moines is at the intersection of I-80 (east/west) and I-35 (north/south). Because of the darkness and weather, you mistakenly took I-35 north instead of I-80 east. You, like me, let out an expletive or two, and quickly turn around at the next exit. And within just a few minutes, you're back on I-80, once again heading east toward your goal, The Big Apple.

Did you quit your journey and head back to California because you temporarily went in the wrong direction? Of course not. You might have become a bit afraid, but you make a course correction and keep going.

Fear is one of many signs along the road on your journey to life mastery. Neither good nor bad, when you're on course, all is well. Make fear work for you and recognize it for what it is: nothing more than a very precise feedback mechanism to keep you aligned with your life's purpose. Off course, or out of alignment with your heart's journey, just consciously follow the signs back in the direction of your dreams and desires.

*The wise man in the storm prays to God, not for safety from danger, but deliverance from fear.*
*– Ralph Waldo Emerson*

Fear provides instantaneous feedback to being in or out of alignment with your life's purpose, and although we spend an inordinate amount of time focusing on our fears, the fact remains that in the physical world, fear does not exist. Fear has no point of origin, no physical qualities, is not born, and does not die. Even if you were to dedicate your entire life to the pursuit of finding a quantifiable commodity labeled "fear," regardless of where you searched in the universe, you would fail. Fear cannot be found.

*FEAR is an acronym in the English language for 'False Evidence Appearing Real.'*
*– Neale Donald Walsch*

Fear, darkness and cold don't really exist. In nature, darkness is the absence of light, cold the absence of heat.

Fear, even on the most primal level, is the absence of well-being, a response – feedback – to a real or perceived threat, and nothing more.

Initially, clients argue, "Fear is real because I experience it."

Yes, and you also experience darkness and cold. And I know, fear can be terrifying, and cold painful. And, of course, that's true. Yet, what is also true is fear is only feedback for something else; the darkness is the experience and feedback for no light, and the aching cold is feedback for the lack of heat.

This isn't a science lesson, but an important way to

become aware of your fears and to use those fears as a tool, a stepping-stone, to life mastery, changing your life, feeling good, and following your heart.

When my children were young and afraid of monsters, my wife, Candace, and I reminded them daily that monsters could only exist in their room if they didn't open their closet door. Once the doors were open, and seeing no monsters in empty closets, my children were immediately comforted for the evening. Yet each new day brought renewed fears, and as the daylight faded and night rolled in, the closet doors needed to be opened once again for them to feel safe.

Later, as a teenager, my daughter, Molly, once said she was tired of fighting the scary, frightening, negative thoughts in her head.

"The more I try to struggle against these thoughts, Dad," Molly said, "the stronger they become."

I reminded Molly of the expression, "What you resist, persists," and asked her to tell me the first thing she does when she walks into her pretty lavender and pink bedroom at night.

"I turn on the light," she said.

"And then," I asked, "tell me what you do when you want the room dark?"

"I turn off the light."

"So, why," I asked Molly, "if you want the room dark, don't you turn *on* the dark switch?"

"Come on, Dad," Molly said. "You know there's no such thing as a dark switch."

I asked Molly to consider that the negative, scary thoughts in her head were just like the darkness in her room, and as there's no dark switch, it's impossible trying to get rid of that darkness without more light.

"I get it, Dad," Molly said, smiling. "I'm trying to fight my negative thoughts as if I could flip off a switch. Instead, if I focus on what I really want, all I need to do is turn on the light, and the darkness disappears."

Smart kid. Less darkness. More light.

*I have not ceased being fearful, but I have ceased to let fear control me. I have accepted fear as part of life, specifically fear of change and fear of the unknown; and I have gone ahead despite the pounding in the heart that says, turn back, turn back, you'll die if you venture too far.*

*– Erica Jong*

## Fear's Flip Side

Consciously and deliberately choosing one less fear-based thought or action is always a huge step. It's never easy looking at your fears, although you must if you choose to follow your heart and practice life mastery.

Observe your fears, and don't engage them. Examine your fears as though you are a scientist. No judgment, criticism or labels. Imagine you're a journalist or a detective investigating your fears. Keep a *Fear Journal* and have fun, asking yourself questions like, "Well, tell me, when did you start developing this fear of door handles?" Or, "Have you always been afraid of dark roads?" Or, "Now you're a smart guy, so why do you start panicking when you have to give a speech?"

Develop the habit of detaching from your fears, observing them as though you were watching a sporting event or game. Become a spectator to your fears, not a participant.

I've met many highly conscious, spiritual masters, from Bangkok to Mumbai, the jungles of Mexico to the mountains of Colorado, Africa to Greenwich Village, the Vatican to Montreal, Canada. Every one of these consciously elevated people lives his or her life with frequent fears and negative thoughts and emotions. What makes these masters different from you and me are not what they think or feel, but how they detach from their thoughts and feelings, and through their intense process of internal observation, either act or not in accordance with their heart's purpose.

Once you've examined and listed a fear, become aware of the flip side to that fear, the desired feeling when aligned with your heart's path. Fear doesn't feel good, so use the experience to understand the other side of what you're feeling, and become conscious of where your heart's path is pointing you.

Become aware of both the fear and the flip side to that fear, and write them both down.

For example, one entry may be:

Less: I fear wild animals.

More: I enjoy nature and walking through the woods.

Less: I am afraid of death.

More: I love my life, and although I know one day my

body will not be here, I choose to focus on the present moment.

Less: I'm afraid I won't have anything interesting to say.

More: I enjoy meeting thought-provoking people and learning new things.

Less: I'm afraid of being close to someone.

More: I'm ready for the love affair of my life, and willing to be transparent and vulnerable.

Less: People will laugh at me if I try to sing.

More: I feel happiest when I'm singing in church.

When you truly examine your fears with the intention of finding the aligning feedback to your life's purpose, you'll make wonderful discoveries.

*Become a spectator to your fears, not a participant.*

For example, a well-known journalist, Rick,* was deathly afraid to fly. For Rick's whole life he simply said, "I'm afraid of flying," and for someone whose job had him traveling in planes of all sizes, helicopters, and private jets, he spent a tremendous amount of time unhappy and afraid. I suggested instead of giving his fear one label – fear of flying – that he breaks down the different aspects of his fears. His list included a fear of being in a closed environment, being out of control, a fear of heights, and in the event of an emergency on a commercial aircraft, not being able to maintain his macho image in public.

Using each separate fear as feedback, Rick made long lists of the exciting things the counter experiences pointed to, including a love for travel, reporting from exotic places, meeting everyday people with great stories, flirting with the flight attendants, flying first class and in private planes, and one day learning to fly a helicopter. Once he knew the flip side to his fear, he consciously chose less of thoughts about what made him afraid, and more of the things he loved and that made him happy.

Sometimes, though, fears are deeply rooted, and require more than self-awareness exercises to heal. It's not uncommon to discover unresolved psychological issues when choosing to follow your heart, leading to the counsel and support of a mental health professional. Choosing to confront PTSD, sexual or physical abuse, addiction, anger management, and other sensitive issues, is a good thing. The road to life mastery has many turns and is never traveled alone. If you need professional help, get it.

There is a flip side to all your fears. Every fear, large or small, realized or unexamined, contains valuable information.

When I started creating this book, I found every excuse possible not to write. Although *One Less. One More.* was already alive inside me, I resisted the passion and excitement of writing a book, simply because I was afraid.

And yet, every day I consciously chose to acknowledge one negatively-based excuse or fear and let it go, while at the same time, allowing one more feeling of excitement and possibility to permeate my being.

For example, using One Less, One More, as a tool, I examined my fear of not being good enough, and I wrote,

"Less: Who am I to write a book?" Once I uncovered the flip side to my fear, I wrote, "More: I've successfully counseled clients my entire adult life and my work truly helps people."

Or, I would fearfully worry and write, "Less: No one will buy this book," which after examining and flipping that to the positive side, I wrote, "More: *One Less. One More.* could reach countless people, in many languages, all over the world."

It wasn't long before I was writing the *One Less. One More.* chapter outline, and then filling in the outline with content, ideas and examples. Despite a nagging doubt that I couldn't possibly write a book, I consciously chose not to engage my fear. I doubted less, while persistently following my heart more. And now, I happily share my book with you.

Your ability to be happy and pursue your heart's dreams and desires is no different than mine or anyone else's on this planet. You were born to follow your heart. Period.

*Fear never comes first. The intention to succeed, to be happy, follow your heart and live life according to your purpose always comes before fear. Because your spirit is infinite and eternal, nothing – truly no-thing – can ever come before your heart's desire, and that certainly includes fear.*

## Take It Slow

What happens when you actually start changing your life and following your heart?

Will you become excited, energized and motivated? Or, will you resist, shut down, and find countless ways and reasons to fail? Like most, you will probably experience both.

There is no telling how or when you will first become conscious of your heart's calling, but you can be sure it will happen. And when it does, your first reaction will be joy and excitement. Your next reaction will be resistance and fear.

You will never be absent of fear, so don't try, and certainly don't kick yourself when fear returns. Observe fear and choose less attachment to it. Instead, choose more awareness of the feedback fear provides, and instantly experience being solidly back on the path to fulfilling your dreams and desires.

*The only difference between a winner and a loser is that the winner gets up one more time.*
*– my grandfather, William G. Vorhaus*

The desire to change your life, be happy and follow your heart *always* comes before fear.

*All* fear is a reaction – resistance – to something else and always temporary. What is true and everlasting is your life's purpose, your desire to be happy. From birth, you emerged to fulfill your purpose, from the formless into form, and nothing – truly, *no-thing* – can ever come before your heart's desire, and that certainly includes fear. Every moment of your life, for the rest of your life, is simply feedback, a response, to whether you're aligned or not with your heart's purpose.

# Use Doubt

*Skepticism is the beginning of faith.*
*— Oscar Wilde*

Questioning is good. Yet, knowing when enough is enough is essential. We all experience the trap of over-thinking. Extreme doubt, when you start questioning even the most commonsensical of circumstances, is a form of fear, a lack of trust for what your heart knows is true. Choosing less doubt releases you from the grip of overthinking, and on the flip side, moves you farther down life's path with just a bit more heart-centered awareness.

Khalil Gibran, the Lebanese-born philosopher wrote, "Love and doubt have never been on speaking terms."

Meagan* is a thirty-something entrepreneur with a huge smile and a magnificent idea for a new service business. Meagan came out of a major automotive company, knew the ropes of the auto industry, and had a tremendous network of friends and resources from both her undergraduate and business schools. Yet Meagan was wracked with doubt.

"What if I can't make it on my own?" Meagan confided. "What if I can't raise capital and articulate my idea? I doubt that I can be a good leader."

When it comes to outward appearances, Meagan is positive and upbeat. When it comes to herself, she is racked with doubt.

I gave Meagan an assignment: Choose just one doubt a day, and when you of think it, consciously become aware of the underlying fear, and using that awareness as feedback, confidently choose a physical action that feels good and aligns with your heart's purpose.

When Meagan caught herself doubting that she could write a good business plan, she switched to remembering, while earning her MBA, the hours spent learning to write a successful plan, and that a leading professor at the school said she could always call for advice.

When Meagan caught herself doubting she could raise the capital for her start-up business, she pivoted her thoughts to the incredible potential her business offered. Using doubt as feedback, Meagan focused on her many business school friends who had already raised funds for their ventures, the relationships she had worked so hard to build in the venture capital community, that she had already demonstrated *proof of concept* for her business, and that several family members had already given her their vote of trust by offering to invest in her new venture.

Once Meagan got in the habit of becoming aware of her doubt, and consciously pivoting to awareness, she was able to use her fears and doubt as feedback and guidance, moving her in a more positive direction, rather than impeding her success.

*Don't let what you cannot do interfere with what you can do.*
*– John Wooden*

Doubt is resistance, an extension of fear. To doubt means you question everything with a negative, fear-based filter, and is *always* a projection of failure. When afraid of being disappointed, doubt imperceptibly creeps in to your thought process, causing you to stop dead in your tracks, and often giving up before you've even started.

How does this feel?

"I doubt you can do that."

"I doubt I can jump that high."

"I doubt she will ever love me."

"I doubt we will win."

"I doubt I'll feel better by the prom."

"I doubt this will work."

"I doubt they will wait for me."

"I doubt they will hire me."

"I doubt I can raise the money."

"At my age, I doubt I'll ever be in good shape."

"Without a college education, I doubt I'll ever be promoted."

"I doubt the engine will start."

"I doubt that would be a fun vacation."

"I doubt you'll find what you're looking for."

The list is endless.

In a CBS Sunday Morning interview, award-winning actor, Chiwetel Ejiofor, explained why he came very close to turning down the starring role of Solomon Northup in the 2014 Academy Award-winning Best Picture, *12 Years a Slave*, "I felt something that I didn't expect to feel, actually, which was just self-doubt. I just wondered if I could tell the story, and I felt the responsibility of it. I felt intimidated by it, actually."

Use doubt as more feedback, another sign of being off course and out of alignment to following your heart. Doubt is not a roadblock. Recognize doubt as an extension of fear, note it, and then consciously choose less of it.

## Why Worry?

Worry is the mask of fear, the slow torture of a frightened mind.

Unchecked, worry is scientifically proven to produce insomnia, allergies, changes in body temperature, chest tightness, constipation, depersonalization, depression, diarrhea, difficulty learning, dizziness, fainting, fast heart rate, fatigue, gastritis, headaches, high or low blood pressure, hyperventilation, impaired concentration, impaired memory, irritability, Irritable Bowel Syndrome, lower back pain, muscle tension, nightmares, palpitations, restlessness, shaking, short attention span, stomach upset or dizziness, tremors and twitches, to name just a few things that never feel good.

And although counterproductive to everything we know as spiritual and beneficial to our health and well-being, we continue worrying. Why? Because expressing worry is wrongly accepted as care and compassion, with the mistaken belief that the habitual act of worry can change or prevent something from happening, which it can't.

Although well intentioned, parents, teachers, authority figures, friends and others, spread their own worry like a contagious virus, infecting you with warnings like:

"Be careful, you can slip on the ice and break your neck."

Or,

"Have a safe trip and be careful not to get in an accident."

Or,

"It's flu season; don't touch anything at the movie theatre."

Or,

"Do you know what the failure rate is for a gay couple?"

Or,

"Darling, you know I love you, but I would be very careful before considering starting that business."

Or,

"I know you really have your heart set on this, but in light of your lack of experience, and limited savings, do you really believe you can succeed?"

Further, listen how the media uses worry to promote a story:

"Coming up, the dangers of walking at night. If you weren't afraid to go out after dark, you may be after watching our next segment. Don't miss it!"

Worry is the fear-based belief that something bad and out of your control will happen, producing terrible results. Worry often begins with, "What if . . .?" and finishes with a future event that won't feel good:

"What if I can't please my lover?"

Or,

"What if no customers come in?"

Or,

"What if my belief in God is wrong, and something bad happens to me?"

Or,

"What if I really can't lose weight?"

Or,

"What happens if I catch a cold and get sick?"

Or,

"What if a terrorist attacks?"

Worrying is another form of resistance to fulfilling your heart's dreams and desires, and choosing less worry is always the correct decision.

Choosing less worry is powerful and transformative, because you are breaking the cycle of unwanted thoughts that don't serve your heart's purpose. Worrying is unhealthy, a present moment projection of something bad happening in a possible future, and, ultimately, creates negative habits of thinking that weaken your ability to feel good and pursue your heart's dreams and desires.

Remember, fear, which includes worry, is feedback, a pointer to what's *not* aligned with your heart's purpose, the reason you were born. Slowly, deliberately, incrementally, break the habit of worry by catching yourself thinking a fearful thought, and consciously switching to the flip side of the equation, and what does feel good.

For example:

When you start going down the dark, fearful side of the "What if . . .?" game, switch to a fabulous, believable and achievable conclusion, such as,

Less: "What if I run out of money?"

More: "What if I cut some expenses and create just 10 percent more revenue, I'll give myself one additional year of cash flow?"

Less: "What if I get sick and can't fulfill my obligations?"

More: "What can I accomplish by staying healthy, eating well, exercising regularly, having regular physicals, and practicing a more holistic mind, body and spiritual lifestyle?"

Less: "What if I never find a mate?"

More: "What if I truly was born to be happy, and remain excited at the prospect of finding someone to share my life? For now, I'm going to enjoy every day of my life while staying awake for the synchronicity of meeting my soul mate."

Less: "What if I fail my test?"

More: "What is the best grade I can earn if I study, do my extra credit and prepare for the test?"

You will never eliminate fear, doubt or worry, because you need the feedback. Have fun, catch yourself when your thoughts don't feel good, and enjoy flipping to thoughts of love, adventure, possibility, peace, happiness and gratitude.

Choose less worry.

## Believe

The American writer Truman Capote said when he was nine or ten years old in Monroeville, Alabama, that he was walking down the road and, "just knew I was going to become a writer, although for the life of me, I didn't know how."

Right now, it's not essential you know how you're going to be happy, achieve life mastery, follow your heart, or realize your goals, dreams and desires. What's important, though, is that you *believe* it's possible, and if you so choose, can always, in every moment, consciously move in the direction of your passion.

Belief is the mental experience of *knowing* before you take the first step of *doing*. Believing you can be happy and follow your heart is the conscious act of disassociating from your fears – the resistance – and connecting with your heart's calling.

It's impossible to comprehend the countless life events that transported you from birth to this moment. Nor can you imagine how the universe will fulfill your heart's desires tomorrow. Yet, to follow your heart, and move forward on your life's journey, you must *believe* you were born to be happy today.

Believe more every day that you were born to follow your heart. Believe you have an important purpose, and that you were intended to be here, now. Believe your life has meaning and each day is a gift. And believe you are here to make a difference.

Again, don't worry about how you're going to be happy, that will come. Just believe – even for a moment at a time – that your life's purpose is to follow your heart, be happy and fulfill your dreams and desires.

Spend more time each day believing.

Believe in miracles.

Believe in the impossible.

Believe in the wisdom of nature.

Believe in goodness.

Believe that you can.

Believe in excellence.

Believe in abundance.

Believe in joy.

Believe in being well.

Believe in love and light.

Believe in exceeding your wildest dreams and expectations.

Believe your life has purpose.

Believe in your body.

Believe in the magic of the present moment.

Believe in life mastery.

Believe in yourself.

Choosing even for a moment to believe you were born to follow your heart and be happy creates enough space in your habitually negative thought process to allow a very powerful seed to be planted deep within your soul. Like an acorn at the moment of germination, when the awakening of the mighty oak begins, your choosing to switch from fear to believing in your heart's calling is the birth of an incredible journey.

When over time you are able to choose less fear and more belief in being happy and fulfilling your true life's purpose, you can relax and connect with the universal inspiration and creativity already within you.

Believing, though, is only the fuel for your heart's journey, not a guarantee of the outcome. Believing doesn't make it so, but it sure helps. Without believing, though, how can you even begin to fulfill your dreams?

In this moment, there may be no empirical evidence you are ever going to become a dancer, ambassador, surgeon, sports commentator, or teacher. Consciously believe it so, and move more in that direction.

There is no guarantee you are going to get well, become wealthy, resolve your family issues, get the promotion, or lose weight. No one can promise going back to college for a nursing degree, or MBA, or earning an electrician's certification, is going to benefit your career. Just because you hope a check will magically arrive, or that your boyfriend will come home, or that the bank will approve your mortgage application doesn't make it so.

Yet, by choosing less fear, doubt and worry, and instead, making a conscious switch to believing in your goals, dreams and desires, while at the same time, continuing to show up every day to do the work, greatly improves your chances for success.

You have only one guarantee: You were born to follow your heart and be happy. And after that, the choice to follow your heart and believe you can achieve your goals, dreams and desires, will be the greatest adventure of your life.

# It Takes Courage to Follow Your Heart

"Why me?" you may ask. "Who am I, out of billions of people on the planet, to follow my heart, do what I love, and believe I was born to be happy?"

"Who am I to believe I can run this city, food co-op, business, or healing center?"

"Why do I think people will buy my art, eat my food, wear my glasses, or shop in my store?"

"Who am I to believe I can succeed, beat this sickness, ever get out of debt, find a life partner, make a billion dollars, or follow my dreams?"

The more courageous question to ask is, "Why not me?"

One conscious moment of introspection can yield huge lifelong benefits; simply by breaking old patterns of disbelief, and courageously believing – knowing – that you are meant to be here, and that your life has meaning.

Courage is not something you do. Once you decide to follow your heart, it's who you are.

Deuteronomy, the fifth and final book of the Jewish Torah, says in verse 31:6, "Be strong and of good courage, do not fear nor be afraid of them; for the LORD your God, He is the One who goes with you. He will not leave you nor forsake you."

In 1955, Rosa Parks, a forty-two-year-old African American woman, riding on a bus in Montgomery, Alabama, courageously refused to give up her seat for a white woman.

Mahatma Gandhi courageously led India to civil rights and independence, ultimately losing his life to the cause, as did the courageous American civil rights leader, Dr. Martin Luther King, Jr.

Jesus was courageous, as was Mother Theresa and Anne Frank.

These are courageous people from the news and history. Yet I know hundreds, maybe thousands, of people who, just like you, choose courage daily.

In far away places, brave troops stand guard, moving across foreign lands to protect and uphold the principles of freedom. In hospitals, doctors and nurses bravely subject themselves to illness and disease to save lives. Teachers courageously inspire their students to light the flame and not curse the darkness. And alone at night, police officers and other first responders intrepidly patrol so we may sleep with a sense of safety and security.

*One isn't necessarily born with courage, but one is born with potential. Without courage, we cannot practice any other virtue with consistency. We can't be kind, true, merciful, generous, or honest.*

*– Maya Angelou*

One rainy day in Brooklyn, I witnessed New York Police Department officer, John Cassillo, courageously chase a would-be assassin into a dark hallway, only to find himself alone and cornered with a Smith & Wesson 9mm gun filled with hollow-point "cop killer" bullets pointed at his head. The bad guy's gun miraculously failed, and Officer Cassillo swiftly arrested the man, single-handedly pulling him outside into the sunlight, where backup support was waiting. Officer Cassillo was lucky, yet how many other courageous cops have not been so fortunate, and despite the job's inherent dangers, continue risking life and limb to protect and serve?

Nancy, a music teacher here in Sag Harbor, courageously spent weekends apart from her family and friends to follow her heart, and become an ordained minister. And celebrity chef Wolfgang Puck followed his heart as a teenager, leaving his home in Austria to work in Paris as an apprentice, and at twenty-five, courageously came to work in America.

It takes courage to live alone after a broken marriage or a partner dies. It takes courage to leave traditional medicine to become an energy healer, cut up your credit cards, or face cancer. It takes courage to change professions, or admit you're an addict and check into rehab. It takes courage to learn how to drive a stick shift, become an actor at sixty (or twenty), or move to another country. It takes enormous courage just saying for the first time, "I love you."

It takes courage to lead when you've always followed, and it takes courage to step off a path that's no longer working. And it takes courage to stand up for what you believe is right and true. And for many, it takes courage just to face each new day.

Consciously choosing to follow your heart and be happy is profoundly courageous.

# Fear to Awareness

CJ\* is a highly respected head college basketball coach, yet for several consecutive seasons he and his team were off their game. Because of some unfortunate personality conflicts within the school, alumni and community, CJ was given the option of either resigning or being fired.

It was a Wednesday afternoon when Tom,\* the school's athletic director, called me about CJ's pending termination, and asked me to fly out the following morning to assist the school. Depending on CJ's choice, the school's leadership asked that I assist in making this termination a calm and honorable process.

"CJ's been more than a coach for us," Tom said, over the phone. "He's an ambassador for our school. This is not going to be easy."

Over the course of his career, CJ had only three professional jobs: A high school head basketball coach, an assistant college basketball coach, and now, a national college championship-winning head coach.

Standing at 6'5", CJ is legendary for his crew cut, impeccable dress and quick wit.

Later that night, I spoke to Coach CJ on the phone. He was totally freaked out and at first intensely angry, which quickly dissolved into abject fear.

CJ had never been fired from a job, enjoyed a steady paycheck, defined himself by the team he coached, and was *always* in control. Now he was beginning to panic; afraid of losing his reputation, fearful that he wouldn't find another job, and uncertain how his wife, Bitsy,* and their   children would perceive him.

We talked long into the evening, and at one point I asked CJ if Bitsy was still awake, which she was. I told CJ to find a quiet place with Bitsy, and as I knew they were devout Christians, to spend some time in prayer.

I also suggested that before praying, they do two things:

First, I told CJ to make a list of all of his fears as it related to this event.

And, two, I told him to use that list as feedback for following his heart's path, and to write down his awareness to what those fears pointed to.

Forty minutes later, both CJ and Bitsy were back on the phone.

"Our prayer took longer than the list," CJ said. "Seems like all my fears are pointing to the dream life we've been planning for quite a while."

"Tell me," I said.

"We've always just wanted three things," CJ said. "A house on the water, a city that has four distinct seasons, and I want to coach a team into the Final Four."

"Coach," I said, "Do you believe in your heart-of-hearts that you can have those three things?"

"Yes, son, I do," CJ said, emphatically.

"Well, Coach," I said, "It looks like the school just gave you that opportunity. Have you made a decision about your termination?"

CJ replied, quoting his bible. "Jesus said, 'Take heart; it is I. Do not be afraid.' Tomorrow, I will respectfully resign."

We hung up, and getting almost no sleep, I took a 5:00 a.m. flight, arriving on campus around 8:30 a.m. The rumor mill was already churning, and I spent the morning working with the school's leadership preparing for the noon press conference at the athletic center.

Walking across the perfectly manicured grounds, I arrived at the athletic complex just as CJ arrived.

Getting out of his shiny Chevy pickup truck, CJ looked great in his brilliant white polo shirt, cleanly pressed khakis, and sharp-pointed, black Arditti alligator boots.

Surrounded by the media, CJ smiled as he walked inside, and responding to the reporter's questions, kept repeating, "It's a good day."

The press event went off without a hitch, CJ resigned, and the athletic director, Tom, publicly repeated the school and community's gratitude for CJ's coaching.

One young, unpleasant, college reporter raised his hand and, trying to unsettle CJ, disrespectfully asked, "Coach, do you feel like a failure?"

The room grew quiet and tense.

"Son," CJ said with a smile. "I love Jesus Christ and He loves me. I've got my health, I've been married now for twenty-two years to my best friend, and I am the father to the most wonderful children in the world. For more years than I could have imagined, I got to coach some of the finest college basketball players on the planet, at one of the finest learning institutions in the world, in a town that is one of America's best-kept secrets.

"Now, young man, I don't know what you're doing

when this press conference is over, but me, I'm walking out that door, grabbing my wife, getting in our truck, and heading on down the road to our next big adventure. Thank you."

And with that, CJ walked off the stage to a thunderous standing ovation.

Within seven months, CJ was appointed head basketball coach at a major northeastern school with four distinct seasons. He and his family now live in a lovely home on the water, and although CJ's team still hasn't earned a spot in the Final Four, I have no doubt they will soon.

# Start Now

*There are no secrets to success. It is the result of preparation, hard work, and learning from failure.*
*– General Colin Powell*

If babies were adults, they would never walk because their initial failure rate is so high. Yet written in a baby's DNA is the command, "Stand up and walk," and despite repeated spills, tumbles and falls, somewhere between a child's tenth and fifteenth month, he or she is walking.

Remember this: the same voice encouraging the baby to walk, is the same voice telling you to follow your heart, be happy and confidently move in the direction of your goals, dreams, and desires.

How long have you allowed the voices in your head to stop you from following your heart? (Too long.)

How does it feel when you listen to others tell you why you can't do something? (Bad.)

And when is the right time to let go of your fears and resistance, and allow yourself to follow your heart? (Now!)

Write on your calendar, paint on the wall, send yourself an email, or scratch it into a piece of stone: "My life's adventure to follow my heart begins now!"

It doesn't matter where you're going, or how you'll get there, or even what it will look like once you arrive. What's important is coming present; providing your heart's purpose with a home, a place of origin in your conscious mind, and creating a physical marker announcing the onset of your life's true adventure.

Don't worry if you say this now, and then again in two months, or two years. Every moment is a new creation; an opportunity to explore the vastness of your potential as it unfolds now, because this present moment – the now – is the only moment there ever is.

Consider this: This very moment is the intersection, the meeting point, the confluence, of where your heart, mind, soul and body meet your past, present and future. Let that sink in. This moment, right now, is your jumping off point from what was, to what is to become.

Mastering your life is about consciously, slowly, deliberately and incrementally, following your heart, doing what you love, and making the decision to be happy. And now, starting today, embrace your fears, worries and doubt, seeing them as nothing more than signs – feedback – along your life's journey. And, at the same time, also choose to courageously believe you are worthy, capable and deserving of being happy and traveling the path your heart desires.

So, what are you waiting for? It's time to prepare.

# One Less. One More.
# Steps

1. Start now.
2. Come present.
3. Consciously choose to follow your heart, be happy and change slowly.
4. Today, consciously choose at least one fear, note it, detach from it, and let it go. One Less: Fear.
5. Today, become aware of something you would love doing, and courageously believe you were born to fulfill that dream. One More: Awareness.
6. Celebrate your progress.
7. Repeat tomorrow.

**One Less. One More.**

# Four

## Prepare

**Less:** Ego
**More:** Heart

*By failing to prepare,*
*you are preparing to fail.*
*– Benjamin Franklin*

**One spring day,** as I was preparing my organic vegetable garden for planting, I had an epiphany. It was a cool afternoon, and my garden looked terrible, still bearing the scars of a brutal winter on the eastern end of Long Island. I replaced broken deer fencing interlaced with dead vines, I turned the weed-filled soil into the garden beds with fresh, black compost, and in shallow, prepared rows, I started planting frost-resistant mesclun, radish, carrot and pea seeds. I caught myself feeling worried that to an outsider, my garden looked barren and dreadfully beaten down, reflecting on me and my gardening skills.

In my heart, though, the chaos of the present-day garden was irrelevant, because my dirty, highly directed, and intentional preparatory work allowed me the first physical opportunity of the season to experience what would eventually become my garden's abundant harvest.

When I saw the garden through my mind/ego's eye, I thought, "What are people going to think of my messy garden?" Or, "Are my friends going to think I'm a gardener wannabe?" Or, "Why am I working so hard when no one cares about my garden?" Or, "This is back-breaking work. Aren't I better off just buying this stuff in the grocery store?"

I knew these thoughts were all from the ego, because it was all about me, me, me.

By catching myself, and consciously shifting to less thoughts from the negative "me" perspective, to more feelings from my open, loving heart, my resistant and unpleasant thoughts of having to work so hard, transitioned to feeling good, knowing I was producing organic food for my family, friends and neighbors. By shifting my thoughts from my head to my heart, and continuing the unhurried, deliberate gardening work with joy and optimism, I was preparing both the garden and, ultimately, my spirit for a bountiful harvest.

Your turn.

At least once a day, consciously observe if your self-centered ego, or enthusiastic heart, is directing your thoughts and activities, because here's the reality: To follow your heart, your life cannot be controlled by the ego.

# The Illusion in Your Head

What is the ego?

For our purposes, the ego is simply personal feedback, your heart's counter-balance, the mind's image of yourself.

Just as a picture of a mountain is not the physical mountain; nor is an image of your dog the actual, living, cuddly pet; nor is the car advertisement the actual car you drive to the market; your image of yourself – the ego – is not really you. Thoughts from the ego may feel like you, but even as the most luscious, inviting, mouthwatering photograph of an ice cream sundae can't be eaten, the ego is only a reflection, a representation of who you think you are. Like a captivating, compelling movie that feels real while you're watching it, the ego is nothing more than a masterfully crafted illusion in your head.

How many times have you watched a scary movie, only to remind yourself, "It's only a movie?" The same is true when you catch yourself thinking habitual, negative, self-centered, fabricated concepts and images, and say, "It's only the ego."

Like fear, the ego is neither good nor bad, just feedback along your path.

Now, in preparation for life mastery, following your heart and being happy, you must consciously take control away from the illusions of your ego, and slowly, gently, intentionally, give more control to your heart.

This is not going to be easy. The ego believes it is *always* right, and will fiercely defend its position. The ego will judge others as wrong and you right. The ego will listen less to others and talk more about you. And, with the option to choose a problem's solution, the ego will choose what it thinks is best for you, often at the expense of others. When the ego is in control, you attempt to win at all costs, attempt to be recognized even when it doesn't matter, and in many situations, the ego will try to demonstrate that you are better and have more than others. When you allow the ego to be in charge, you stand in the epicenter of your world, and everyone and everything else is in some varying degree on the outside. In effect, if you believe and follow the illusion of the ego, you will feel separate and alone.

*In the nineteenth century inhumanity meant cruelty; in the twentieth century it means schizoid self-alienation.*
*– Erich Fromm*

The ego is terrified of death, and fights to stay in control. The ego by its very nature is temporary. When the body's time is over, the ego doesn't survive. Your heart, your spirit, is eternal, although everything else in form, such as our bodies, the sun, trees, bugs, ideas, prejudices and the ego, are born, live and, ultimately, die.

The ego lives in fear. Everything the ego tries to convince you is real, is not. The ego is afraid if you *let go and let God*, a common expression in the recovery movement, something bad will happen, and you will cease to exist.

The ego's common theme is, "You're either with me

or against me." The ego encourages anger, resentment, and complaining, reinforcing its position as the arbiter of what's correct. The reality, however, is that the ego is only a temporary voice in your head with absolutely no power, except the energy you give it.

Your life's purpose, and who you are as a spiritual being, is separate from the ego.

You are not the ego.

## Who Am I?

When you were conceived, you were pure consciousness and intention. As your cells multiplied you became form, and after nine months or so, you were born.

Your parents gave you an official name that quickly became part of your permanent record. But wait, how could your parents name you before they knew you? Did your name become you, or did you grow up becoming your name?

Your name became your very first label, your first introduction to the process of separation and the appearance of your self-image. Ask your parents why they didn't name you Zuma, Jago, Goncalo, Muffi-Jo, or Lettice, which, by the way, are real first names. You were named as the image of what someone hoped you would grow up to become, a projection of someone else's belief system, but not because of who you truly are.

As you grew older, parents and society added more filters, labels and attachments to your image, which eventually became more pronounced: "your ancestors were slaves," "the rich are criminals," "boys act differently than girls," "greedy people don't do this," "good girls don't curse," "our family always does that," "stand up straight," "don't ask questions," "our God is the only God," and "walk this way."

Soon came the teen years, resulting in dismissing your parent's wisdom in search of your own identity. You kept your given name, but switched from doing what your parents wanted, to talking, dressing and acting like your friends, who in turn acted like their friends, who are all, ultimately, manipulated by the media's messages of not being good enough, which directly feeds the ego's insatiable hunger for *always* wanting more.

The ego creates markers for various stages of your life, and you blindly accept these collective labels as truth for how you're to be perceived, such as, "I am a *millennial, newlywed, childless, smart, baby boomer, unemployed, middle age, empty nester, rich, retired, or old*," to name a few. These isolating distinctions are used by the ego as an excuse to either feel temporarily better about yourself, or, in most cases, worse.

All of these filters, layers and labels align with the ego's illusory images, not your true life's purpose, your authentic heart.

As feedback, think of the ego as resistant thoughts, anything that provides either a positive or negative emotional charge by comparing yourself to something else, such as, "I am right, you are wrong," "I have more than they do," "I have less money than you do," "I am stronger than she is," "Compared to my friends, I am fat and unattractive," "She is prettier than I am," or, "I was here first." For the ego, it's always about "me."

Your body – your Earth suit – and everything about your physical nature, including your name, is all just a temporary vessel for this life's journey, and like your ego, is here to serve you, not the other way around.

> *The ego is not master in its own house.*
> *– Sigmund Freud*

Here's your choice: You can either live in a self-centered, negative and fearful illusion, with the ego's endless resistant chatter about lack, something missing, something better, something wrong, or not good enough, or you can follow your heart and live life filled with extraordinary wonder and magnificence, feeling the joy and peace of knowing that all is well in every moment, starting now.

You are complete and connected to the entire universe, and your true nature is to fulfill your life's purpose and be happy. It's really that simple.

# The Ego Report and Your Spiritual Physical

To better understand the ego, try this:

Write down, "The ego says I am . . ."

Under that, write your full name.

Now under your name, write your age, sex and

occupation. Also write the name of the street where you grew up, one fear, one passion and your political affiliation.

Next, write three people you feel superior to, and three people to whom you feel inferior.

Also, as though you were on a first date, write your three best, and three worst qualities.

Finally, write anything else you believe best describes who you truly are.

Let's call this "The Ego" report.

Look at what you wrote. Is it accurate? Is The Ego report who you truly are?

Let's find out.

Start by looking in the mirror. Look hard. Is there anything in the reflection that defines you, the name you call yourself? Is there anything there that gives clues to your name? Is there anything in the mirror that would tell a total stranger you are the person you just wrote about?

Do you look Republican? Democrat? Do you look gay? Straight? Without any clothes or uniform, is there anything in the reflection that might tell another person you are a police officer, architect, nurse, seminarian, truck driver, student, sales manager, programmer, celebrity, brain surgeon, teacher, mom or activist? Can you tell if that person in the mirror came from a broken home, the Southwest, or was raised by a single parent? Is there any clue in that image of yourself to being superior to the garbage man and your ex-wife, or to being inferior to a rich movie star or a happily married mother with four children? Can anyone tell by looking at you the name of your siblings or parents, your secret passion, purpose in life, favorite fruit, or your exact birthday?

The answer to all these questions is "no."

Okay, let's go deeper and try to find you.

We'll ask Dr. Awakening to give you a physical.

Dr. Awakening starts poking around both inside and outside your body, looking into every orifice, organ and system. Will Dr. Awakening find a ticket, sticker, or pointer, some identification connecting you to the person in The Ego report? Again, the answer is "no."

So, now let's allow a scientist, Professor Enlightenment, to take a few cell samples from each of Dr. Awakening's tests, and examine you down to the cellular level, even down to a sub-atomic level. And what does Professor Enlightenment find? He, too, finds no evidence of the person you described in The Ego report.

What's going on? Where are you? Who are you?

*You are not a thing, a body, an object, brand, label, or an opinion. You are spirit, a piece of heaven, part of divine intelligence, and connected to everything in and around you. You are the power that beats your heart, breathes your breaths, and coordinates trillions of actions within your body at this very moment. You are without boundaries, without definition, and without limits. You are a magnificent expression of everything that is, ever was, and ever will be, in the entire universe.*

If you follow the ego, the scared, negative voice in your head, the idea of being connected to the universe is a joke.

If you follow your heart, the belief that you are an endless, vibrating energy form connected to the entire universe, resonates in truth.

To prepare for life mastery, and do what you love – the fulfillment of your dreams and desires – learn to discern the difference between the voice of the ego and your heart, and consciously choose to move forward less from the ego, the separate "me" and more from your heart, the connected "ours."

In order for the ego to remain in control, you need to protect and defend your identity, ideas, concepts, beliefs, country, family, roles, religion and more. The ego protects your story and labels, lives in the world of competition, and *always* wants more.

Sometimes, results of the ego, such as being promoted (over someone else), getting a raise (over someone else), winning a race (over someone else), building a bigger house (over others in the neighborhood), marrying the stud or bathing beauty (over others) or being named, "Best in Class" (over others), feels great. Yet, everything experienced through the ego is always temporary, and to continue feeling good, the ego wants more. To change your life, be happy and follow your heart, you must demote the ego to a simple feedback mechanism, not a controlling authority. Once aware of the ego, you have no choice but to either leave it in charge, or start moving command of your life more to your heart.

Left unchecked, the ego will try to rule your life, working very hard to convince you that you are best alone and separate from the universe and all humanity.

Everyday, in continued preparation for fulfilling your heart's dreams and desires, consciously choose less influence from the ego, and more guidance from your heart.

## Why Prepare?

Success favors the prepared, which is why the military, security and medical personnel, along with crisis professionals like me, spend hours in preparation and training for myriad, unthinkable events.

On a kayaking trip in Maine, our L.L. Bean guide, Suzanne, made us practice various procedures in the event our kayak tipped, or we lost sight of our group on Casco Bay.

"Just because what we are practicing today has never happened," Suzanne said, "it's important we prepare for the future when it does."

Prepare daily for the heart-centered changes in your life by consciously and deliberately taking a step back and, without judgment, simply observe if your thoughts and actions are directed by your ego or heart.

Imagine firefighters arriving on the scene of a raging fire and spending time reading the manual on the proper use of the attack hose. Or, arriving on set for the first day of a movie shoot, the star doesn't know his lines. Or, at the start of battle, an Apache helicopter pilot has to stop and learn how to fly her new piece of equipment. Or, during an essential one hundred and fifty feet dive, a professional deep-sea diver checks his gear for the first time minutes before going under water. Or, while apprehending a fleeing criminal, a police officer must first call headquarters for the proper procedures on applying handcuffs.

Before teachers begin their school year, they've already prepared their entire year's lesson plan. Successful actors spend hours preparing for an upcoming role by actually living in the world their fictitious character portrays. Nature photographers spend weeks in preparation for that one perfect shot; preparatory – prep-schools, prepare students for a successful college experience, and my clergy friends admit their worst sermons always follow not being prepared.

Preparation may already be part of your life. You prepare for family vacations, business meetings and first dates. You prep your lawn before seeding, prepare your home before a party, and prepare and practice your presentation before a shareholder meeting.

And now, as with all great journeys, once you choose to follow your heart, be happy, do what you love, and, ultimately, change your life, you must prepare.

Captain Paul J. Brown of the New York Fire Department agrees.

At the beginning of his career, Captain Brown followed his heart and his grandfather, father and two brothers – one a surviving 9/11 first-responder – and joined the New York Fire Department, the busiest combined fire and emergency medical services organization in the world, second in size only to Tokyo, Japan.

Captain Brown told me, "As a professional firefighter, I've learned that preparing for a life filled with purpose and passion is like professional gambling. Most people tend to focus on likelihoods, then make their choices on what they feel is probable.

"Consciously choosing to following your heart and do what you love, and intentionally preparing for a passionate, satisfying life, changes the odds in your favor, because you are now increasing the number of likelihoods, the possibilities for achieving your heart's dreams and desires.

"Sure, we all have dreams, some attainable, others seemingly unattainable. Yet in both my personal and professional experience as a veteran NYFD firefighter who prepares for emergency events and successful outcomes daily, success in life is based on believing what your heart tells you is true, and then moving about your day in conscious preparation for the fulfillment of those dreams."

## Trusting Your Heart

*Trust yourself. You know more than you think you do.*
*– Dr. Benjamin Spock*

Our first child, Connor, was born a month premature. I was with Candace when he was born and felt something was wrong.

I told Candace, and, although neither one of us had

experience with newborn babies, she said, "Follow your heart and tell someone."

Off to the next birth, our doctor had already left the room. Trying to keep cool, I told the nurses I sensed my son was having some sort of difficulty.

One nurse turned to me and asked sarcastically, "Oh, are you a doctor?"

"No," I said. "It's just a feeling."

"Well," she said, "look around you. You're in one of the top hospitals in the world, and your son is being taken care of by some of the finest medical professionals anywhere. Don't you think if something was wrong with your son we would know? Just relax."

I followed the nurses as they took Connor upstairs to the nursery. Watching him in the crib, I knew, really knew, that although he looked fine, he needed help. I asked another nurse to check on him, and she, too, said he was fine.

In my head, my ego was telling me that I was overreacting, that I should trust the authorities, that I didn't know enough to comment on my son's health, and that if I kept pushing, the doctors and nurses wouldn't like me. My heart, however, was telling me to get help.

I made a frantic call to the hospital's pediatric department, leaving a message on their voice mail to please have a doctor come look at my son. I felt so foolish because there was nothing externally to indicate a problem, but my intuition – my heart – told me my newborn son was in trouble.

I went back down to be with Candace, feeling confused and anxious. What if I was just overreacting? What did I know? I'd never been around babies before and this was just a feeling, and nothing more.

Thirty minutes later, a leading pediatrician from the hospital, along with a group of interns and nurses, walked into our room looking very serious.

"We've moved your son to pediatric intensive care," the doctor said, "and he'll be there a while. Because he was born premature, his lungs are not fully developed, and we missed it. He's going to be all right now, and I truly apologize. But, Mr. Vorhaus, the larger question is: How could you possibly have known Connor was in danger?"

I explained that it was a gut feeling.

"Thank God you trusted your intuition," the doctor said, "because at the end of the day, there's nothing more powerful than a parent who follows their heart."

How *did* I know? I'm not a doctor, had no experience with these things, and Connor looked fine. Yet consciously choosing to listen less to the negative noises in my head, and more to the clear calling of my heart, I unmistakably heard, "Get help for your son."

Gradually allow your heart to open, learning to trust your intuition more, because over time you will become astounded at the vast amount of information endlessly available to you from the unseen. Trusting your heart enough to quiet the critical voices in your head, opens you to wisdom far beyond what your five senses can perceive.

**One Less. One More.**

Trusting your negative thoughts less, and your heart more, requires you to listen carefully, to hear beyond the sounds of the ego's very convincing resistant voice. When you trust your heart, even your silence is full of possibility and inspiration.

Trusting your heart more allows communication from your higher guidance in ways unimaginable to the ego.

When you trust your heart more than the ego, you walk less in fear, tense, defensive, or worried, which gradually opens an unencumbered path toward realizing your dreams and desires.

I love the story of the little girl walking through the woods with her father, and as the sun starts setting behind the trees, the young child announces her growing fear of the dark.

"Don't worry, my darling," the father said, "Let me hold your hand."

"No, Daddy," replied the little girl. "Let me hold your hand."

"What's the difference?" asked the father.

"Well, I'm small and you're big," said the daughter, "and if something happens, I may not be strong enough to hold your hand. But I know, Daddy, that you are so strong, and if something happens, you'll never let me go."

Consciously choosing to trust your heart more than your ego blesses that exact moment. By trusting your heart, you release your grip on being small, separate and alone, and immediately connect to your greatness, your ability to create a life filled with joy and abundance.

Golda Meir, Israel's former Prime Minister said, "Trust yourself. Create the kind of self that you will be happy to live with all your life. Make the most of yourself by fanning the tiny, inner sparks of possibility into flames of achievement."

Prepare for your life's journey by relying less on the ego, and more from your heart.

The ego is fearful, limited, and ultimately, temporary. Your heart is endless, eternal and dedicated to your happiness and the fulfillment of your life's purpose.

The ego says, "I want to find happiness." Your heart says, "I am happiness."

The ego says, "This is mine." Your heart says, "This is ours."

The ego says, "Shut up!" Your heart says, "I'm listening."

The ego says, "I want more." Your heart says, "Let's share."

The ego says, "Damn you." Your heart says, "Bless you."

The ego says, "I'm better than you." Your heart says, "We can do this together."

The ego says, "I am right! You are wrong." Your heart says, "You have an interesting point of view, let's consider both sides."

The ego says, "I want sex now." Your heart says, "How can I please you?"

The ego says, "I'm the head of this household." Your heart says, "I'm a contributing member of this family, how can I support you?"

The ego says, "Fight!" Your heart says, "Peace."

# Never Alone

*If ever there is tomorrow when we're not together, there is something you must always remember.*

*You are braver than you believe, stronger than you seem, and smarter than you think.*

*But the most important thing is, even if we're apart, I'll always be with you.*

*– A.A. Milne,* Winnie-the-Pooh

It takes time learning to discern the differences between the voices in your head and the calling of your heart, which is why, as you prepare to change your life, it is essential you involve a trusted mentor. All remarkable journeys, including yours, come with unforgettable mentors that provide the wisdom, knowledge, confidence and resources required for your heroic passage into the unknown. And don't worry, if you think you don't have a mentor now, you will very soon.

In Greek mythology, Odysseus, prior to leaving Ithaca to join the Trojan War, asked his dear friend, Mentor, to take charge of his son, Telemachus. Over the years, Odysseus's wife, Penelope, persistently fought off unremitting suitors as she waited for Odysseus's return.

After many years, the goddess, Athena, disguising herself as Mentor, encouraged Telemachus to stand up to his mother's suitors, and go off in search of his father to bring him home. Athena was, literally, Telemachus's trusted Mentor.

Mentors, both in fiction and real life, become the external voice of your heart's calling, the expression of intuition, destiny, experience and truth. Mentors are the teachers, guides, and if in your belief system – spirits and angels – that provide the guidance, information, direction and confidence needed for your exciting adventure ahead.

Mentors also provide the spirit imbued amulets, charms, potions, bracelets, coins, lodestones and deities, which contain the essence of your heart's strength, wisdom and all your life's possibilities.

Mentors represent the voice of your heart, your source energy, the divine, such as Obi-Wan Kenobi (Alec Guinness) in the movie, *Star Wars*, when he tells Luke Skywalker (Mark Hamill), "The Force will be with you, always."

Oprah Winfrey credits her fourth grade teacher, Mrs. Mary Duncan, as one of the most influential people in her life.

"A mentor is someone who allows you to see the hope inside yourself," Oprah said in a 2002 interview on Boston TV. "A mentor is someone who allows you to know that no matter how dark the night, in the morning joy will come. A mentor is someone who allows you to see the higher part of yourself when sometimes it becomes hidden to your own view. I don't think anybody makes it in the world without some form of mentorship. Nobody makes it alone."

Most often, older, wiser and more experienced, genuine mentors have your best interest at heart. Through your mentor's wisdom, counsel and more important, their belief in you, you feel protected, and in many ways, you are. Having one person you trust implicitly to focus specifically on your success and well-being provides tremendous comfort and relief, especially when through experience, that person knows the potential dangers and obstacles ahead.

In Amherst, Massachusetts, local baker and organic farmer, Ben Lester, the co-founder of the popular non-GMO bakery, Wheatberry, and creator of the nationally recognized Pioneer Valley Heritage Grain CSA (community supported agriculture), credits his late father as his mentor.

"As a Harvard-educated mathematician, my father analyzed everything, including me," Ben said.

"Although my father died when I was twenty years old, he taught me to follow my heart, and that regardless of any obstacles, if I stayed true to my passions, my life would be successful. As a husband, father, farmer and businessman, I carry his belief in me as a constant reminder to never waiver from my heart's path."

"If I only had a mentor," clients will often tell me, "I wouldn't have made those mistakes." Or, "With a mentor I could have achieved more." Or, "I never trusted or respected anyone enough for them to be my mentor."

Through the years, many clients lamented over not having one specific trusted teacher or mentor, using what they perceive as their lack of mentoring support as an excuse for failure or not achieving their goals. Even without a material mentor or teacher, they, like so many, discount the endless sage advice they receive from both the physical and non-physical realms, including the daily mentoring from non-traditional teachers, such as a boss, spouse, sibling, child, neighbor, a stranger, or even their own intuition.

For centuries, Western culture has perpetuated the belief that once you leave your childhood home and become an adult, you are essentially on your own. Furthermore, another common belief is that once your life is over, and you take your last breath, your death is a solo act, and you die alone.

This is such a terrible thought it's no wonder so many people are afraid to die. The good news is that nothing could be further from the truth.

Not all mentors are physical. From the instant universal energy enters your mother's womb, bringing your life's creation into form, until the moment your heart, soul and mind's non-physical energy merge back into its wholeness, you are connected to a universal spirit, your true mentor, and always under the loving care of infinite guides and teachers.

For the rest of your life, regardless of whether you have a physical mentor or not, you have unlimited instant access, 24 hours a day, 365 days a year, to the most magnificent mentor and guide in the universe: your spirit, your heart.

I remember one early morning after a terrible night's sleep fraught with worry, I cried out, "God, where are you?" And without a moment's notice, I heard back in a strong, deeply connected voice, "I am here. Where are you?"

I realized by listening to the negative voices in my head, I had let worry and fear remove me from the present moment. Yet when I was able to come present, and listened to my heart, my true mentor, I was not alone.

While alive in this physical body, you will continue discovering new and extraordinary guides, teachers and mentors, in both the physical and non-physical realm alike. As you continue trusting your heart more, you will be amazed at the signs, symbols, metaphors, people and situations that appear seemingly from nowhere, pointing you in the correct direction, at the appropriate time, as you passionately navigate life's journey.

*When the student is ready, the teacher will appear.*
*– Buddhist proverb*

Choosing to follow your heart takes on new meaning when you realize everything you've ever sought externally in a mentor is already present and alive deep within you.

Confucius, the Chinese philosopher said, "Wherever you go, go with all your heart." Jesus said, in Matthew 28:20, "I am with you always." And from the Bhagavad Gita, "The power of God is with you at all times . . ."

Trusting your heart won't replace physical mentors, teachers and guides, although it will certainly help you attract the right ones. Here in your heart, deep in your soul, resides the universe's collective wisdom, waiting for expression through your life's experience.

Throughout time, mentors, teachers and guides have

pointed us back to trusting our heart, the eternal truth of our soul's purpose, to experience and express our true nature. Every human being, at one time or another, needs help along the way.

*Why, when a person you wholly trust tells you to take risks, or directs you to travel into unfamiliar territory, you gladly do so with a sense of excitement and anticipation? Yet when you hear the voice of your source, your higher awareness speaking through your heart, you resist and often don't listen?*

In our culture, it takes a tremendous amount of courage to follow your heart, trust your internal voice and live inspired – *in-spirit* – because from childhood, we are taught to trust others over ourselves.

As though in a trance, Buddy,* a famous comedian-actor, sat speechless as he realized that, although his agent, manager, partner, studio head and accountants were well intentioned in their advice, he had become conditioned to following their direction and guidance, while discounting his own heart and intuition.

"I followed my heart when I became a comedian, and got my own TV show. I thought just doing what I loved was enough, and I left the rest of my career to the 'experts,'" Buddy told me. "For years I felt this deep calling from my heart to write a coming-of-age movie, but everyone told me to stick to what I knew: television. After years of wasting time listening to everyone else, I finally followed my heart, wrote and sold the script."

If you allow the ego more control than your heart, your life feels fake, as though you are acting: Acting as a church leader, playing the part of a boss, a dutiful son or daughter, acting as the good wife, the strong husband, the best friend. When not following your passion, your heart, you end up feeling smaller, off-center, off-purpose, and perhaps trapped.

Even with the best of intentions, over the years I've unwittingly tried to get my children to conform to my wishes, and to ignore the calling of their heart.

When Connor was in elementary school, all of his classmates were New York Yankees fans. The kids would often wear Yankee gear, adorn their books with Yankee stickers, and would talk about nothing else but the Bronx Bombers.

Connor, however, choose a different path: he was a New York Mets fan. He got a lot of grief from his classmates, and for one particularly contentious game, knowing that everyone else would be wearing their New York Yankees caps and pinstripes, Connor donned his Mets gear and headed for school. Fearing a backlash, I strongly suggested Connor leave his Mets clothes at home, which he adamantly refused.

"Leave me alone, Dad. I'm following my heart."

That night Connor came home happy. Not only had the Mets won, but it turns out a bunch of his friends were secretly Mets fans, just too afraid to go against the crowd.

# Prepare to Commit

Believe you can run the family business, and prepare for your involvement.

Believe you can raise the money, and prepare for the challenge.

Believe you will solve the problem, and prepare for the resolution.

Believe your life has purpose, and prepare for the direction.

Believe you matter, and prepare to be cherished.

Believe in romance, and prepare to celebrate your new love.

Believe you were born to be happy and follow your heart, and prepare for a new life.

Believe you can go the distance, earn the degree, discover the new solar system, change professions, ace the test, make babies, ride a unicycle, and prepare for what's ahead.

Steadily preparing for life mastery is simply the daily rhythmic process of consciously choosing to follow your heart, believing you were born to be happy, recognizing that fear is just a sign – feedback – along the road, and that by giving less control to the ego, and instead, trusting your heart and intuition more, you connect with your timeless mentors, guides and teachers, decisively, recognizing you are never alone.

Now, it's time to commit.

# One Less. One More.
## Steps

1. Start now.
2. Come present.
3. Consciously choose to follow your heart, be happy and change slowly.
4. Today, choose one less ego-filled, negative, fearful, competitive, resistant, judgmental or divisive thought or action, and let it go. One Less: Ego.
5. Today, choose one more intuitive, spirit-filled, heart-centered thought or action, and embrace it. One More: Heart.
6. Prepare to do what you love, and celebrate your progress.
7. Repeat tomorrow.

## Five

## Commit

**Less:** Procrastination
**More:** Proactivity

> *If you deny yourself commitment,*
> *what can you do with your life?*
> – Harvey Fierstein

**If you, like most**, pause before actually committing to changing your life and following your heart, recognize there is a big difference between hesitation and procrastination.

Hesitation is the moment before you leap in the lake; that momentary flash of questioning your true intentions. Do you really want the thrill of jumping into the cold brace of refreshing water, or would you rather stay dry and sit this one out? You want to jump in, but there's a voice in your head trying to stop you with excuses and images of potentially dreadful outcomes. Although you know the lake is cool, clear and safe, and your friends, beckoning you to jump, are already in and enjoying themselves, you still hesitate.

It seems like such a simple decision, yet you resist, standing at the edge of the water, immersed in an annoying internal conversation about whether or not to go in.

Aware that fear is holding you back, and knowing the flip side to that fear will be the joy of joining your friends, you commit, jump, and for the rest of the day, never once hesitate to jump in again.

Hesitation before a major commitment creates a momentary gap, an opportunity to slow down and reflect on present conditions, observing if your intentions are a reaction to fear and ego's control, or conversely, in genuine response to your heart's dreams and desires.

Hesitation is another form of resistance, a natural feedback mechanism, and an integral part of your internal guidance system. There is a cadence to hesitation, a rhythm, a bridge from one point of action to the possibility of another, and in that moment of pause, what remains is pure intention, the space to either move forward or hold back. It is here, in this seemingly empty space of hesitation, where all potential possibility is born. Claude Debussy, the French composer said, "Music is the space between the notes."

There are times, even after committing to change, that your heart calls you to hesitate, slow down, and momentarily pause before moving forward. Recognize this moment as the end of one chapter, and the beginning of the next. Committing to change creates a new landscape, an entirely original, uncharted world. You are about to enter an unknown realm where few have gone before you, and regardless of your proactivity, any meaningful commitment is a big deal, and not to be taken lightly.

Do not expect one day to wake up committed to change and happiness without some fear, resistance, or hesitation. That works in the movies, not in real life.

*Three things in nature grow quickly: fire, cancer and weeds. For you, opting to be happy and follow your heart is best done gradually.*

If you find yourself resisting, running away, or avoiding the idea of making large, wholesale changes, slow down and trust your instincts, because you're probably moving too fast. Breathe, find your footing, and allow yourself the luxury of pause until you feel comfortable in this new setting.

The expression, "He who hesitates is lost," is not necessarily true.

Hesitating and then choosing not to perform an illegal or dishonest act will keep you out of jail.

Hesitating and then choosing not to get in a car with a drunk driver will save your life.

Hesitating and then choosing not to hurt or destroy a life prevents guilt, regret, and if in your belief system, bad karma.

Hesitating and then not choosing to push a bad legislative bill through simply because of political pressure will, ultimately, make better laws.

Hesitating before spending money you don't have, and

waiting until you have the cash, demonstrates financial maturity.

Hesitating and not having sex with someone who doesn't honor your body is soulful.

Hesitating and not jumping off a cliff without knowing the depth of the water below is wise.

Hesitating and not accepting the wrong job just because it pays well will, eventually, serve your career.

Hesitating before agreeing to a business deal because everything appears in order, but your gut tells you to wait, honors your divine intuition.

If fear is the sign along the road, hesitation is the speed bump.

Procrastination, though, is an entirely different animal.

# Less Procrastination

Imagine you've always wanted to firewalk. You prepare yourself physically, mentally and emotionally for the challenge, and along with one hundred and fifty other brave souls, the night finally arrives. Surrounded by wildly supportive walkers and staff, you watch as each person approaches the ten-foot corridor of fire, and with a loud yell, marches off across the hot, burning coals. Now it's your turn. For a brief, hesitant moment, you consider running the other way. But you don't. Taking a deep breath, you commit to the firewalk, scream, "YES!" and in a matter of moments, you're through the one thousand-degree fire, elated, strong, excited and changed forever.

Conversely, now imagine instead of performing the firewalk, you relinquish control to your fears, step out of line, and tell the group leader, "I'm going to do this later," or, "I've got an important meeting tomorrow and I can't afford to get hurt," or, "This is stupid. I'm not going to do this." How would that feel?

Procrastination is the ego's sly misdirection away from achieving your goals, and never feels good. The size or implication of the task or decision is irrelevant. If you know a thought or action is required for the change you seek, and consciously choose a contrary action, or worse, no action at all, you are out of alignment with your heart's purpose.

Keep track in your journal of the times you feel like procrastinating and what you want to put off. Become conscious of why you feel that way, and observe the choices you finally make. Follow each entry of procrastination with a reminder of your goals, dreams or desires, and how this specific act of procrastination works against your commitment to change, happiness and the fulfillment of your heart calling you to adventure. Have fun with your journal entries, and once you understand the problem, creatively become part of the solution.

For example, are you procrastinating because you believe you work best under pressure? If that's the case, work backwards from the target deadline for completion, chunk out the tasks necessary to complete the action and attach deadlines to each task.

Knowing full well that deadlines or goals may be

jeopardized, procrastination is a trap, a conscious and contrarian decision to stall change. Following your heart is hard enough. You don't need the added burden of procrastination. Procrastination is a veil of fear, and when you catch yourself, like all feedback, you can use these internal delaying tactics to better understand your resistance to change, and discover what is calling you to be happy and fulfilled.

Are you a "people pleaser," and procrastinating because you can't say "no"? Did you decide to work on a project today, but when a friend, colleague or lover showed up, you dropped everything to meet their needs? Make your commitment to change more important than taking care of someone else first. Be available *after* you've completed the task required for the fulfillment of your dreams and desires.

Are you procrastinating because you're a perfectionist, or simply afraid of the unknown? Give yourself permission to make mistakes, and accept that any change can be scary. No one would get anything done if they didn't give themselves permission to make mistakes. Make your passion bigger than fear.

Procrastination is a dangerous saboteur to change, an enemy to happiness.

Break unwanted, negative, stalling habits, by consciously choosing fewer acts of procrastination, and rewire your mind to accept – not reject – more proactive commitment to change.

# Don the Dean

Don* is the dean of a prestigious law school. I've helped Don's school with various communications and crisis issues, and coached Don personally on his communication and leadership skills.

Don graduated magna cum laude from a top eastern school, went on to receive his masters, and then, after moving west, earned his law degree from a top-ten law school. Universally admired and respected, Don, a stocky, bald, African American, is accomplishing great things, both for himself and the school.

Attending an industry conference, Don and I had a free hour and sat together alongside the large, sparking pool at the resort.

In Bermuda shorts and fidgeting with the buttons on his pink polo shirt, Don confided that he felt lost; worried he was going to die without truly following his heart.

"I'm having an existential crisis." Don said. "Although I'm successful, and I enjoy my work, I keep thinking there's got to be more to life than dinner parties, recruitment trips, board presentations, and alumni fund raisers. I just don't know why I'm here, or if I even have a purpose."

Don appeared sad and vulnerable, and I encouraged him to continue.

"Who am I?" he asked rhetorically. "Sure, I'm making a lot of money, and I've reached the top of my field, but so what? I'm committed to my work, yet I know I'm neglecting my own life and family. I am so afraid to take time just for me, and whenever the opportunity presents itself to do something that makes me happy, I find an excuse and put it off until later. Later? When's later? I put off all the fun and personally rewarding stuff to keep myself on a rat wheel."

I asked, "How does it feel, succumbing to your fears, and putting everyone and everything else first? How does it feel putting you and your happiness last?"

"Terrible," he said.

"So, are you willing to change that?" I probed a bit further.

"Of course," he said.

"And will you commit right now to becoming proactive?" I asked.

"Yes," Don said.

"Okay," I said, "What today – in this moment – will you commit to changing specifically for you to become happy and fulfilled?"

"My marriage," Don said without pause.

"Good," I said, "What, in regard to your marriage, have you already put off today?"

"Calling home to speak to my wife, Cindy," he replied.

"So, what's more important," I asked. "Your marriage or your job?"

Don's eyes lit up as he told me about his love and appreciation for Cindy. He went on to express gratitude for everything she does for their family, how she's such a great mom, why they make such a good pair, and how on every business trip Cindy still writes sexy love notes, hiding them in his luggage.

Interrupting himself, Don stood up.

"Listen, man, I hear you. I've procrastinated long enough, and it's time for me to take back this marriage and become more proactive. Before going back into these mind-numbing meetings, and allowing the day to get away from me, I'm calling Cindy."

Fifteen minutes later, Don returned, all smiles.

"Cindy asked if I was having an affair, because I never call in the middle of the day just to say 'I love you,'" Don said.

"And how are you feeling now?" I asked.

"Peaceful, grateful and happy," Don said. "I have a lot of catching up to do for the many years I was emotionally and physically absent from my family. But I'm looking forward to becoming a more proactive and available husband and father."

Become the spectator, not participant, when you feel the burden of procrastination. Observe the reasons you avoid, deny, trivialize or refrain from continuing your commitment to being happy and following your heart, using this feedback as inspiration and motivation toward proactively fulfilling your dreams and true life's passion.

## Commit to Change

Every voyage begins at the moment of commitment.

The ancient Chinese philosopher, Laozi, said, "A journey of a thousand miles must begin with a single step."

Regardless of any fears, resistance, hesitation or

procrastination, if you intend to follow your heart, be happy and change your life, you must eventually commit to the adventure.

Author and management consultant, Peter F. Drucker, said, "Unless commitment is made, there are only promises and hopes; but no plans."

Bill Gates committed to change when he left Harvard University in 1975 to form Microsoft with Paul Allen. Jeff Bezos, in 1995, afraid he had missed the Internet boom, committed to following his heart, and on a cross-country journey with wife, Mackenzie, wrote the business plan for an online bookseller originally called Cadabra, which soon became Amazon.

Maybe you're thinking about leaving a relationship. Or starting a new venture. Maybe you feel it's time to quit an addiction, give up a bad habit, or stop complaining. This may be when you consciously choose more positive thoughts, to only speak with integrity, or admit the lies you've been perpetrating. Now may be when you buy your first boat, move to a new country, contribute to charity, establish an orphanage in Africa, or attend the college of your dreams. Or, this may be when you become serious about changing your eating habits, the way you exercise, the church you attend, your living arrangements, or the way you dress.

*The moment one commits oneself, then providence moves, too. All sorts of things occur to help. A whole stream of events issue from the decision, raising in one's favor all manner of incidents and meetings and material assistance which no one could have dreamed would come his or her way.*

*– Johann Wolfgang von Goethe*

To change your life, you must first proactively commit to the change.

Committing to change is the moment you, or any human being on the planet, takes the very first step into a new reality. Nothing can or will change in your life until you walk through this door. Until you consciously commit to being happy, following your heart, and changing your life, your journey cannot – will not – begin. You will never be able to do what you love until you commit to moving in that direction.

Although it sounds incredibly simplistic, without committing to change, the universe doesn't know what to do on your behalf, so it does nothing and waits.

No relationship can succeed without commitment. No investor will fund your start-up without your demonstrable commitment. A new job without commitment is doomed to fail. Without commitment, success at any creative or sporting endeavor will end in defeat. You may want a new addition to your home, but without committing to the project, it won't get done. Without commitment, you remain awash in a sea of uncertainty.

Mario Andretti, the Italian-born racecar driver said, "Desire is the key to motivation, but it's determination and commitment to an unrelenting pursuit of your goal – a commitment to excellence – that will enable you to attain the success you seek."

From the moment you commit to following your heart, you will be tested, tried and challenged at almost every turn. Expect these obstacles and welcome them. Open your heart to every trial, because with each victory, each new experience on the road to fulfilling your dreams, you will learn, grow and expand far beyond your wildest imagination. Whatever it is you want to happen, whatever change you seek, whatever dreams and desires fill your thoughts, whatever passion burns inside of you, none of it can happen until you proactively commit to the journey and take that first step.

My daughter, Molly, loves sailing, one of the many advantages to living by the sea. As a teenager, Molly and her sailing team often trained in bad weather, and several times a year, she and her fellow sailors ended up in the drink – a sailing term for capsizing their small boats and falling into the cold, dark water.

As a father, I want my daughter safe and protected, and I asked Molly if it wouldn't be more secure to keep the boats moored during squalls. Looking at me incredulously, she said, "Of course, Dad, but I committed to sailing in all weather, and sailboats are meant to sail, not to be tied down doing nothing."

It's time for you to proactively commit to following your heart and set sail.

Do not – and I repeat, *do not* – expect to feel secure or comfortable at this point in your journey. Fighting to stay in charge, the ego will not be happy with your decision to follow your heart, often attempting to create havoc in your mind.

When making the commitment to follow your heart, expect an inordinate amount of fear and resistance to move through your being. Be compassionate, not only to yourself, but to others who, when learning of your decisions and actions to change and follow your heart, will most certainly experience their own fears and discomfort regarding the unknown.

Stay awake and gently observe what this fear is telling you. Spend time writing down both your fears, and the flip side to those fears.

For example:

Proactive: I commit to being happy.

Fear: I can't be happy. No one in my family has ever been happy. I have no right to be happy. How can I be happy when so many terrible things are happening in the world?

Flip side: I was born to be happy. I can be the first in my family to be happy. My birthright is to be happy. My happiness can bring light, joy and peace to the world.

Proactive: I commit to being in a loving, passionate, mentally healthy, long-term relationship.

Fear: Most relationships don't make it, why try? I've never had any luck in relationships. My parents would never approve this relationship. Once this person really knows me they'll leave me.

Flip side: Take time and find someone who shares my values toward a committed and loving relationship.

## One Less. One More.

There's no guarantee in any relationship, but with the right person, the more I give, the better the chances of long-term success. My decision to commit to this relationship is based on my standards, not my parents or anyone else's. I am not perfect, but I know I'm a good person and deserving of someone's love and devotion.

Listen to all the internal and external feedback, and while the ego tries desperately to understand your commitment to a new path it can't yet comprehend, become very aware that your heart and soul remain steadfast, peaceful and calm.

Despite feeling off balance and uneasy about the future, the moment you proactively commit to change, happiness and the pursuit of your dreams, every ounce of your being coalesces to focus on the fulfillment of your goals and desires, because you are now on the exact path you've been searching for, and precisely where you are meant to be. Commitment changes the future.

When you commit to change, you begin a new journey into the unknown, the unexplored. For now, become comfortable with a dark, empty void. Trust your heart and continue walking forward in your commitment to change. At some point in the future, farther down the road, this exceptional path will glow warm and bright, but only because you are the one shining the light.

All great journeys emerge from the unknown. What is hidden in your personal cave? What lurks in the darkness of your inner space? What waits around the corner in the jungle of your mind? The only way to ever discover your personal truth is to proactively commit to change, allow yourself to initially feel off balance and out of control, and, starting from exactly where you are now, take a deep breath and move forward.

So often my clients think just because they have the guts to finally commit to pursuing their passion and heart's calling that the seas will part, harps will play, customers will begin appearing out of the blue, and the universe will reward them with unlimited riches dropped graciously from the sky. Unfortunately, that's not the way it works.

All that happens when you agree to proactively commit to following your heart and pursuing your dreams and desires is that a new story begins. What happens next is the adventure.

## Commit Enthusiastically

*Years wrinkle the skin, but to give up enthusiasm wrinkles the soul.*
*– General Douglas MacArthur*

Animators, mystics, chefs, concrete workers, microbiologists, clergy, healers, tattoo artists, florists, auto mechanics, costume designers, carpenters and others, who share the excitement and passion of their work, captivate me. Often, I'm so drawn to an enthusiastic narrative, that when a person is finished explaining their work, I, too, want to experience that exact job or exhilarating event.

The job you do, the life you live, the relationships

you share are made whole and divine with your passion, commitment and enthusiasm.

Henry Ford said, "Enthusiasm is the yeast that makes your hopes shine to the stars. Enthusiasm is the sparkle in your eyes, the swing in your gait, the grip of your hand, the irresistible surge of will and energy to execute your ideas."

Committing enthusiastically anchors you in the present moment, connecting you to the passion, zeal, exhilaration and excitement of your life's journey.

"Let's go to the amusement park!" is an enthusiastic decision, leading to the thrill of the roller coaster.

"I'm jumping in the frigid ocean on New Year's Day!" is the enthusiastic choice that results in an exciting, unforgettable Polar Bear Plunge in the sea.

And, "Good morning, darling! I just can't help myself: I have to hug you!" says the eager and enthusiastic parent to her children, who will never forget their parent's loving, safe and adoring embrace.

Enthusiasm means *in God*, en + theos, from the Greek, *entheos*, meaning *inspired* – in spirit. Happy sharing the depth of their joy and gratitude, enthusiastic people don't hold back when feeling good. And with poignant expressions of loss and sorrow, enthusiastic people can also move you to tears. Think of enthusiastic symphony conductors, parade grand masters, entrepreneurs, ministers and circus ringleaders. We merrily follow enthusiastic people because their spirit is so big.

Like air filling a flat tire, enthusiasm supplies every

cell with universal life force, infusing your commitment to happiness with the same energy that moves stars across the sky. With nothing more than laughter and delight, enthusiasm creates its own gravity, effortlessly attracting people, events, circumstances and opportunities to you.

Ralph Waldo Emerson said, "Nothing great was ever achieved without enthusiasm."

Enthusiastic commitment births greatness, fuels desire's fire, and feeds passion with the same power that creates heaven and earth. Rising to a level of enthusiasm refocuses your commitment today, allowing you in each moment to create unforgettable experiences for tomorrow.

Enthusiasm is contagious. Before being repressed by a controlling ego, children fill their play with wonder, excitement and possibility. Just listen to a child's enthusiastic story of a frog, leaf, feather, sister or new pet, and you, too, become spellbound.

Today, you know of origami because my great aunt, Lillian Vorhaus-Oppenheimer, whom we called Grandma, committed enthusiastically to introducing every child in America to origami.

In the late 1950s, Grandma traveled to Japan, and after discovering an origami flapping bird, found her heart's calling, and set out to introduce Americans to the Japanese art of paper folding. Returning to the U.S., Grandma enthusiastically immersed herself in origami, and began sharing her experiences with friends, family and anyone else who would listen to her new passion. That enthusiastic commitment landed her on NBC TV's, *The Today Show,* beginning an American love affair with paper folding.

Out of her brownstone in New York City's Greenwich Village, over the following two decades, Grandma established the Origami Center of America, now called OrigamiUSA, and through Grandma's proactivity and commitment, mentored many brilliant origami artists, who themselves, through their own enthusiasm, sparked a movement, creating an origami educational program now taught in almost every primary and secondary school in the world.

"Where is your enthusiasm?" I ask clients when they are describing a new product launch, a major speech, a script they are about to start shooting, or the beginning of a well deserved sabbatical. Inevitably, the resistance to expressing enthusiasm is fear. The fear of how they'll be perceived by others, the fear of how they'll look, fear that their leadership will be diminished, or fear their enthusiasm will be seen as childish or unprofessional. And worse, so many highly educated, successful people resist expressing enthusiasm for fear of "jinxing" themselves. *If I'm too excited, it won't happen. If I'm too passionate, I'll end up being disappointed.*

If you are not used to expressing enthusiasm, go slowly and get used to both the ego's resistance, and the attempted thwarting from others not comfortable with your outward display of delight. Allow your joy to exceed anyone else's negativity.

Look for the resistance to your own enthusiasm, and write it down, because the flip side to that pushback is exactly the commitment your heart is calling you to experience.

Enthusiastically, lead your team.

Enthusiastically, prepare for unknown events.

Enthusiastically, write the business plan for your new idea.

Enthusiastically, give a speech.

Enthusiastically, start each day on set ready to work.

Enthusiastically, challenge the status quo.

Enthusiastically, promote the best person for the job.

Enthusiastically, champion your peers.

Enthusiastically, run in the rain.

Enthusiastically, make angels in the snow.

Enthusiastically, make love under the stars.

Enthusiastically, celebrate the butterfly's arrival in the spring.

Enthusiastically, bid farewell to foliage in the fall.

Enthusiastically, enjoy renewed health and well-being.

Enthusiastically, hug your grandparents.

Enthusiastically, hug your grandchildren.

Enthusiastically, hug a tree.

Enthusiastically, honor your friendships.

Enthusiastically, howl at the moon.

Enthusiastically, dance naked.

Enthusiastically, jump on the trampoline.

Enthusiastically, pray filled with gratitude.

Enthusiastically, start a parade.

Enthusiastically, follow your heart.

Enthusiastically, run up the stairs.

Enthusiastically, lead a standing ovation.

Enthusiastically, support your spouse/children/lover. Enthusiastically, be alive.

Once you've proactively committed to following your heart, every moment, if you so choose, will be filled with unlimited opportunities for surprise, wonder, passion and enthusiasm.

# Take the Leap

Are you ready? Are you sure? Because once you commit to following your heart and doing what you love, choosing to take those first steps into a new, unknown world, nothing will ever be the same again.

Planning for college is different than attending your first class.

Promising to find a new job is different than starting a new job.

Telling people you're going to write a movie is different than writing "THE END" at the end of your finished script.

Discussing the future after a few dates is entirely different than saying, "I love you," for the first time.

Are you ready?

Are you truly committed to following your heart? Then it's time to leave the safety of what you know, and proactively embrace this unfamiliar adventure.

As a child, you felt this moment would come, and although you may not remember it, you started this journey long before you were born. No more procrastination, excuses, or regrets. Once you commit to following your heart, any obstacles in your path will now seem irrelevant compared to the passion you feel welling up inside.

While others may look for the perfect time to commit to change and follow their heart, you know today is ideal simply because it is *now*.

Don't just say it, commit to it. Today, proactively make change real.

Put out the cigarette.

Order the chicken coop.

Sign the check, lick the stamp, and send off the application to art school.

Tell her you love her.

Commit with all your heart and soul to Christ.

Go to AA.

Become kosher.

Give notice.

Say, "yes."

Say, "no."

Put down the sword.

Pick up the broom.

Plant the seed.

Leave.

Stay.

Form a political action committee.

Put on the karate *gi*.

Take off your clothes.

Turn on the lights.

Paint the walls orange.

Apologize.

Fix the door, get a mammogram, move the cash.

Close the deal.

Put down the bagel.

Ask for help.

Study.

Sing.

Dance.

Nap.

Stop.

Go.

If your dream is to play the guitar, just listening to Eric Clapton won't help you. You won't become a better parent by reading a magazine. You can't learn how to make love by watching sex in the movies. Attending a baseball game won't teach you how to hit a home run, nor can you get wet from reading the word *water*.

Until now, everything related to achieving your goals, dreams and desires, was an exercise in faith and preparation for this new journey. Yet the instant you commit to following your heart, being happy and changing your life, and proactively taking action, a new adventure begins.

In this moment, because of your commitment, the universe instantly calibrates for the fulfillment of your heart's intentions, and you launch a new life experience from an elevated, more alive perspective.

The commitment to following your heart also extends far beyond what you can imagine today. Consider the potential impact your courageous decision has on others. How will the world change because you proactively commit to eating healthier, going for the promotion, connecting with your childhood sweetheart, earning your diver's certification, flying around the world, running a bed and breakfast, or getting that dreaded colonoscopy? What new future will you create when you commit to spending more time with your family, learning Spanish, becoming a nurse, biking, lifting weights, volunteering, removing the clutter, writing a song, cleaning the bathroom, discovering a new star, planting a garden, kissing him, adopting a dog, or getting baptized?

Proactively committing to following your heart is not a science, nor is there a roadmap to fulfilling your purpose. The train to your future doesn't leave at a certain time, nor can you miss a flight to bliss. There is no schedule to your achieving life mastery, nor can you do anything wrong.

When you commit to a goal, you move forward. And when you hesitate, you create the momentum for your heart to pause, recommit and continue on, or not. You see, it really doesn't matter, because your heart's calling never stops, and the moment you choose to commit, or for many, recommit, the universe is ready and at your beck and call.

Ultimately, stepping off into the unknown, and enthusiastically committing to change your life, be happy and follow your heart, is a magnificent act of confidence. For many, a proactive commitment to fulfilling your life's purpose is left for another lifetime, because mustering the nerve to move forward with only a vague sense of what the future holds can be daunting at best, and paralyzing at worst.

If you feel exhilarated after committing to following your heart, and then hear a terrified, distrusting voice in your head asking, "What the hell am I doing?" you're in just the right place.

Stand strong, come present and listen to your heart. Force yourself to remember why you're here, and that you consciously chose to change your life, be happy and fulfilled. Although this moment may not feel pleasant, as the ancient Sufi poets taught, "This too shall pass."

Like most commitments, there will be forces, sometimes quite strong, trying to convince you to stop following your goals, dreams and desires, attempting to knock you off this heart-centered path. You may choose happiness, yet the universe is required to confirm your intent.

For maybe a day, a week, month, season, several years, or the rest of your life, the universe will continue challenging your decision to follow your heart. In every story, including yours, this moment is where the hero is required to demonstrate steadfast commitment to achieving the goal.

You are the hero of your story, and before circumstances test you, ask yourself: "How far will I go?"

How far will I go if I believe the government is unfair?

How far will I go in my role as a public servant? Spiritual leader? Teacher? Activist?

How far will I go to be closer to my children? Parents? Guru?

How far will I go to save my marriage?

How far will I go to be the boss? The CEO? The

founder?

How far will I go to be someone's friend? Mentor? Advocate? Protector?

How far will I go to no longer live a lie?

How far will I go if I fall in love again?

How far will I go to write a book? Stage play? Business plan?

How far will I go to save animals? Improve national literacy? Fight global warming?

Or, how far will I go to get well? Heal? Get straight? Walk again?

Be ready for the universe to ask, "How far will you go to change your life, be happy and follow your heart?"

How far will you go to do what you love?

How committed are you to achieving your dreams and desires?

How much do you really want this?

How far will you go?

Because once you stop procrastinating and make the commitment, you need to let go.

# One Less. One More.
# Steps

1. Start now.
2. Come present.
3. Consciously choose to follow your heart, be happy and change slowly.
4. Today, choose one less procrastinating thought or action, and let it go. One Less: Procrastination.
5. Today, proactively commit, or recommit, one more enthusiastic thought or action to ful filling your heart's dreams and desire. One More: Proactivity.
6. Do what you love. Celebrate your progress. Have fun!
7. Repeat tomorrow.

# Six

## Transition

**Less:** Control
**More:** Experience

*One doesn't discover new lands*
*without consenting to lose sight*
*of the shore for a very long time.*
*– Andre Gide*

**Imagine your childhood dream** is riding *The Beast* at Kings Island in Mason, Ohio, one of the longest, fastest, wooden roller coasters in the world.

Consumed by the vision, you commit to the adventure. You save the money, take off the time, fly to Cincinnati, rent a car, drive forty-five miles northeast to Kings Island, buy your ticket, get in line and maneuver yourself to sit in the best place on the ride: the front seat of the front car. You've done everything you can. Now what?

Let go, and experience every glorious moment of this magnificent roller coaster.

The intention you set was to ride The Beast. What you're

wearing is irrelevant. What other people on the ride think of you holds no significance. Your religion, social status, or education means nothing now. Nothing from your past or future can or will change anything while you wait for the ride to start. No financial, relationship, career, or health issues have any influence on what's about to happen. You spent years imagining this moment, followed your heart, set your intention, believed one day you would achieve this moment, prepared, committed, and now you have only to strap in, sit back, take a deep breath, come present and let go!

In the next instant, The Beast releases from the gate, beginning its long, slow, noisy, click-click-click-click ascent up the 110-foot hill, to then free fall 135 feet at 65 mph into an underground tunnel, and for the next breathtaking 4 minutes and 10 seconds, you're left screaming with delight, knowing your dream has come true. You did it!

Life is the roller coaster. You're here to ride.

Although it sounds counter intuitive, once you commit to being happy and following your heart, you will spend less time trying to control life, and more time experiencing it. There is, however, a catch: To experience anything, you need to be present. You cannot experience something tomorrow, yesterday, in an hour, or next year. Every experience, including mental, physical, emotional and spiritual, only happens now, in this moment, which is really the only moment there ever is. The past is gone. The future hasn't yet arrived. There is only now. To be happy, change your life and follow your heart, you must become proficient in the transitional, incremental, life-long practice of coming present and letting go.

Letting go of control, and practicing being present, is a natural transition for anyone on a passionate, heart-centered, path. Still, letting go is rarely easy. For a mother to experience birth, she must release her baby from the womb, beginning a lifetime progression of letting go; first when she surrenders her toddler to socialized play, then to a formalized education system, and, eventually, independence, when her child leaves home. To be healthy, your body naturally eliminates waste. To successfully begin a new relationship, you must first let go of the one before. A trapeze artist can't fly without letting go of the bar, you can't make a purchase without letting go of your money, and at one point, at the end of this life, you must let go of your physical body. All essential transitions happen only after first letting go.

Even if something isn't working, such as a destructive relationship, an illness, a non-productive job, or even an old, broken car, you still, at one time, infused this object with your energy and attention, and the transitional process of bidding it farewell equates to releasing a part of yourself, producing an innate sense of loss and melancholy.

Still, to transition into a life filled with passion and wonder, you must first let go of the past, and slowly ease into the unknown.

The mysterious excites and awakens your heart. Conversely, your self-image, the ego, believes it is empowered to control and protect every aspect of your life, including the past, future, people and events around you, creating a constant, low-grade buzz of insecurity. If allowed, the ego will aggressively attempt to control the universe, and it will always fail. The unknown terrifies the ego.

Although physically impossible, the ego tirelessly endeavors to play God, not relaxing until it feels that everything is in its place, which it never completely is.

The ego believes that to achieve success, you must compete, judge, consistently acquire more, and relentlessly control the world in and around you. The ego is wrong. Do you control your heart beating? Digestion? Cell structure? Do you control the growth of your hair or fingernails? Do you control the next time a bird flies by your window, or what someone's going to say on the TV? Do you control the sunrise, your neighbor's political beliefs, your sister's sexual orientation, or when your boss will next text you?

Here, then, is the dilemma: For the rest of your life, while your heart wants to come present, let go, expand, explore, experience and express every glorious moment, the ego wants to tighten its grip, hold on and control the impossible.

In the Bible, Proverbs 16:33 says, "The lot is cast into the lap, but its every decision is from the Lord." Though you physically throw the dice, you can't systematically determine how they fall.

Remember, the ego is simply a feedback mechanism, a sign along the road. The ego's job is offering resistance to your life's purpose, the counter-balance to your heart's calling. To consciously follow your heart and be happy, gradually let go of the ego's attempt to control the world, and instead, transition to coming present, allowing yourself the magnificent experience of this very moment.

*God, grant me the serenity to accept the things I cannot change, courage to change the things I can, and wisdom to know the difference.*
 – *Reinhold Niebuhr*

# Transition

Transitions are imperative to becoming strong, confident and happy. Transitions are rarely swift or painless. You cannot, nor should you, expect a quick, effortless transition to following your heart, changing your life and achieving your goals.

Children let go of living in their parent's home when off to college. College graduates let go of school's structure to begin a new life and perhaps a new career. Couples, when they commit, let go of their life alone to join a partnership. A new manager lets go of the familiarity of a task-driven job for the promotion to a management function. New recruits on their first day in the armed forces are required to let go of their hair and civilian clothes for a uniform. And Native Americans, beginning their ceremonious Vision Quest, symbolically let go of their childhood after completing intense time alone in the woods.

Once you consciously choose to change your life, you must let go of what you've always known, and experience the gradual transition to a place you've never been. Although you know deeply in your heart that you're headed in the right direction, there's still a part of you that's freaking out. That's normal.

Imagine two streams flowing toward each other down opposite sides of a mountain. This convergence creates white water, resistance and turbulence, although the streams eventually let go of their individual nature to form a larger, formidable river, now powerfully heading in unity to the sea.

Transition includes the moment you stop fighting the river and join it; the process of becoming the person your heart called you to become. In all journeys, transitions are the moment of tension, that point in time where change is prevalent and in motion, where what was, is no longer, yet what is to be, is yet to come.

Transition is what our family calls "the in between," the place where you've begun letting go, although not quite having fully landed in your new home. Give yourself an enormous amount of credit; it takes a brave soul to continue on through any transition.

Breathe, quiet your mind, and sense your peaceful heart. What you are experiencing through this transition is both normal and naturally required for lasting change. Even food requires heat and time to complete the transition from raw to cooked.

Imagine the metamorphosis of the caterpillar's changing form, not completely emerged as the butterfly, and wrapped in the strange, disorienting darkness of the cocoon. Transition creates the flow, the natural movement, the neutral space of significant change.

Transitions express universal realignment, the measurable space between the change from child to adult, worker to boss, single to married (and married to single), childless to parent, manager to leader, minors to majors, renter to owner, addict to sober, incarcerated to free, and ego-based to heart-centered.

All transitions are both exciting and scary, specifically because you now must give up your old world, and start fresh surrendering the past and an ego-filled projected future, for the experience of this very real, heart-filled, present moment.

Nicolas Rousseaux, a leading expert on corporate transitions, advises companies through the often traumatic transition of a merger or acquisition.

Nicolas told me, "To be in any transition, whether corporate, personal, professional, or spiritual, is like being in the middle of a desert. You know you are crossing something huge, although your passage is fraught with major doubt and few possible choices but to move forward. Regardless of who you are, how much money you have, whether you're famous, or what your position in life might be. When in a transition, you have only one true choice, and that is to let go and keep pushing on."

Transitions are life's shifts, the change of clothing, the darkness just before dawn, and the momentary space between breaths, musical notes, and the *beats* between story scenes.

Stay true to your dreams and passion, because the ego is totally out of its league, feeling neither safe or secure. Your heart understands this tempering of your soul; it's the ego that's resisting.

Watch for the feedback. As with all transitions, the ego will masquerade as negative thoughts, fear, anger, frustration and worry. These obstacles will be waiting like bandits in the dark corners of your mind, hoping they can break you down, move you off course, or get you to run off screaming, panicked, afraid and ready to quit. Don't engage; just observe, and flip the ego's feedback on its ear. Do this and you'll quickly come right back to feeling your heart's passion, knowing you remain aligned exactly to your true life's purpose.

Everyone I've worked with – truly *everyone* – including world leaders, the wealthy, athletes, entrepreneurs, politicians, military and security personnel, religious leaders, celebrities and everyday people alike, when faced with transitions, revert temporarily to a place of fear and uncertainty.

The very capable president of a large country told me for the first couple of months in his new job, he was nearly paralyzed with fear, waking up every morning worried that he would be exposed as a phony. "This is scary stuff because it's all real-time, on-the-job training," he said, after realizing there's no such thing as president's school.

A popular school superintendent of a mid-sized city was being considered to run one of America's top school systems. He was about to voluntarily remove himself from consideration because, as he told me, "I'm not sure I'm ready for the leap." He was more than ready, just scared. And a beautiful, young actress, just breaking through as an A-list movie star, told me she was never more stressed and anxious in her life. Why? "Because," she said, "I don't know that I deserve or can handle this."

When I was twenty-three-years-old and working at a radio station in Des Moines, Iowa, I was offered a better job opportunity at another radio station in Kansas City, Missouri. One Saturday, I drove south on Interstate 35 for the interview, and was hired on the spot. Yet, after leaving the interview and driving around Kansas City, which was almost four times the size of Des Moines, I remember thinking, "There's no way I can make it in a city this big." Thankfully, I did not give in to my self-limiting fear, took the job, and had a blast.

Still, just because you choose to change your life and follow your heart doesn't guarantee you instantaneous success or the immediate realization of your dreams. Like a new pair of shoes, it takes time – sometimes, quite a while – before your heart-centered life becomes comfortable. Stay strong and confidently move forward, knowing your heart and all your higher guidance is wisely leading you to the right place, in just the right time.

Be aware though; to the ego, change and transitions represent death, and will fight to stay in control. Expect to be off balance, afraid, unsure and skeptical of your path. Just don't quit. I repeat (and repeat it to yourself): Do not give up!

Transitions are fraught with uncertainty, anxiety and the constant fog of the unknown. Yet, through this haze, you will emerge victorious, as have most soul travelers before you.

Does this feel familiar? Believe me, you are not alone.

*Life is pleasant. Death is peaceful. It's the transition that's troublesome.*
– Isaac Asimov

## The British Brothers

Through the years, I've worked with two very successful British brothers.

The oldest, Nigel,* is a media maven and a classic control freak. Everything for Nigel is, "My way or the highway."

His younger brother, Andrew,* is an internationally recognized, award-winning musician, who never lets anything or anyone bother him. Andrew has several close friends, and millions of fans. Creating a recording studio near his home, Andrew spends all his free time with his wife and children, always traveling together. Andrew's two loves are his family and his music, and he awakes every morning with the attitude, "Today is a new day, and I can't wait to see what music comes through me!"

On the other side of London, brother Nigel works very hard to create the perfect life for himself: The trophy wife, a stunning flat overlooking Hyde Park, the proper private schools for his children, the best Savile Row tailor, the perfect address for his media empire, and a stunning, discrete, young mistress.

Nigel is known at the finest restaurants, always travels first class, and has just the correct number of influential friends in government, education, sport, entertainment, publishing and British nobility, to make for the ideal dinner party. When you talk to Nigel, everything is always, "the biggest," "the best," "the most important."

For Andrew, the musician brother, although rich and famous, he doesn't attach to material trappings, and as his wife and a team of professionals manage his significant finances, he's not interested in knowing his net worth. Andrew generously gives to charity and donates his name and time to meaningful causes, always encouraging his family and friends to do the same.

At one point, Andrew's life continued getting better, while Nigel's life started falling apart.

Nigel's became an emotional mess during a period when his business began suffering, his marriage unraveled, his children wouldn't talk to him, and the British gossip columns were reporting false, sordid tales about his life. The more Nigel tried to control his wife, parents, children, employees, media, the competition and friends, the more frantic he became.

Nigel tried keeping everything in its place, yet few aspects of his life complied.

"What do you really want?" I asked Nigel. "What, in your quiet moments, brings you joy just thinking about it?"

"I want to be more like my brother," he said. "I don't want to manipulate my life and the world around me to be happy."

I asked Nigel to list all the things about his brother that he valued. Surprisingly, Andrew's fame and fortune didn't make the list. The top five items that Nigel admired were: 1. Andrew lives in the present moment and is always relaxed; 2. Andrew's family adores him; 3. Andrew makes a good living doing what he loves; 4. Andrew doesn't worry about the future; and 5. Andrew is usually happy.

I suggested for one week Nigel observe his obsession with control and keep a journal.

Nigel was shocked. From the minute his eyes opened in the morning, until he took his sleeping pill at night, he attempted controlling everything. His list was enormous, and we were both astonished at Nigel's habitual controlling behavior.

"Bloody hell," Nigel said, "Who do I think I am, God?"

Out of sheer relief, we both started laughing uncontrollably.

I advised Nigel to consider three things. First, I suggested he seek a professional mental health counselor to deal with his underlying fear and anger. Secondly, as I knew both brothers, I arranged a weekend retreat where Nigel could reconnect with his brother and learn more about Andrew's life philosophy, and why he is so often happy. And, third, I suggested once a day Nigel consciously let go of one act of control; and conversely, allow himself one more present moment experience through the prism of gratitude.

Nigel continues practicing One Less, One More, except he says for him it's, "Many Less and Lots More."

Nigel sees his mental health therapist once or twice a month for what he calls, "tune-ups." Hiring smart leaders, he doesn't have to micro-manage, his business is again thriving, and, although Nigel's marriage failed, he stopped seeing his mistress for a more meaningful relationship with a lovely woman from the Cotswolds.

Nigel's children are slowly rediscovering their father, and Andrew's children are growing closer to their uncle. Nigel no longer takes sleeping pills, his new apartment is simple and cozy, and, although he still travels first class, he never again indignantly asks a service person, "Do you know who I am?"

The best part: Nigel and Andrew have never been closer.

"I still want to control life," Nigel told me recently. "I just know for my heart to be happy, I need to let go and experience more of my life today."

# Existential Crisis

It may start as a low hum that builds to a roar. Or you may suddenly be overcome with overwhelming feelings of alarm. Or, for just a moment, find yourself frozen with awe. Regardless, somewhere along this journey, you will experience an existential crisis.

Although there is no one-size-fits-all resolution to an existential crisis, when feeling alone and questioning the meaning of life, try this straightforward exercise to help you return to center.

## Come present.

*Focus on your breath, your heartbeat, the person sitting across from you on the subway, the door to the microwave oven, the petals of a flower, the flight attendant's eyes, a cloud across the sky, anything that fixes your attention to this present moment. Say to yourself, "Hello. I am here."*

## Become aware.

*Repeat several times, "All is well. All is well. All is well." Even if you don't at first believe it, consciously hear yourself say the words, "All is well." Remind yourself that you are an important part of an extraordinary universe, and although you don't have all the answers, and may be feeling afraid or uncomfortable, your life is an adventure, and your heart's purpose, the reason you were born, is to be happy. Period.*

## One Less.

*Consciously choose one thing, and one thing only, that is upsetting you. "Why am I here?" "What is my purpose?" "Who am I?" "Is death the end?" "What is the meaning of life?" "Am I alone?" "Does anything really matter?" "What if I get fired?" Once you've isolated the negative thought or emotion, carefully and with great curiosity, observe the many ways that thought or feeling has controlled you. Remind yourself that what you are observing is only feedback, thoughts in your head, directing you toward a desire from your heart. Now, less under the control of feeling bad, detach from that controlling idea, and holding for a moment in your mind's eye, consciously and deliberately let it go.*

# One More.

*Continue staying present and choose one thing, and one thing only, that appears to be the flip side to your upsetting, controlling thought or emotion. So, if your question is, "Why am I here?" stay present, observe that you may be feeling alone, worthless or unappreciated, and flip it to how you want to feel, such as, "I am loved," "I am worthwhile," or "I am appreciated" or "I am here to follow my heart and do what I love." The moment you choose not to be controlled by negativity or fear, and instead, consciously choose to come present and align with your heart, you can experience more of your authentic transition from fear to peace, negativity to joy, ego to heart.*

# Celebrate.

*Remind yourself that the only way to have an existential crisis is, by its very nature, that you exist; you're alive, and here now. Be grateful, and remind yourself that all human beings at some point in their life feel this way, and it's perfectly normal and okay. Remind yourself, too, that all your thoughts and emotions are simply part of a glorious feedback mechanism, and in every moment, you still have the authority to consciously choose less of what makes you feel bad, and more of what makes you feel good, the true path to change, happiness and life mastery. End by repeating, "All is well."*

# Let Go of Regrets

*A man is not old until regrets take the place of dreams.*
*– John Barrymore*

During a bitter divorce battle, Jeff* lamented not marrying his high school sweetheart instead of his soon to be his ex-wife. He regretted relocating to California instead of moving back closer to his Midwest hometown. Jeff was also convinced had he gone to a better college he would have become the CEO for a larger company, and had his financial advisor given him better advice, his options for retirement would be different.

I suggested Jeff consider letting go of his regrets and commit today to become a more compassionate leader, a more approachable father, a dynamic community participant, and more physically active, the life changes he knew would make him happy.

"I have no regrets!" Jeff replied defensively, "I just wish things had turned out differently."

What do you regret?

Regrets are subtle forms of resistance, the ego's attempt to remain in control and keep you rooted in past events that cannot be changed, misdirecting your attention to a time that no longer exists. Feeling powerless to the past, festering regrets cloud your ability to fully commit to following your heart, resulting in a mental, murky fog, which never seems to completely dissipate.

Our family understands the grip regrets have on keeping us from being happy, and every New Year's Eve we practice what we call *The Regret Box Tradition.*

Just after dark on December 31st, we light a big, roaring fire, and our children, family, friends, business colleagues, neighbors and anyone else in tow, gather around our fireplace with the intention of burning all our regrets.

Privately, and for as long as it takes, everyone writes down his or her regrets, both large and small, past and present. Every regret is personal and confidential, and the more regrets written down, the better.

My regrets often include not spending enough time with my family, demonstrating intolerance, projecting my fear into a situation, or becoming conscious of something unpleasant I've held on to from my past. I write them all down.

Prompting our friends, Candace and I ask random questions, such as, "What do you regret from your twenties?" or, "What in your relationships do you regret?" or "What do you regret about your body?" or "What do you regret about a recent failure?"

Often, at the beginning of the Regret Box exercise, some guests proudly proclaim, "I have no regrets!" And then they start writing one regret after the next, soon realizing how much negative energy they've been holding inside.

When everyone's done, we fold all the lists, placing them in a cardboard box, and, after covering it, ceremoniously throw the Regret Box into the fire, collectively yelling, "Regrets, be gone!"

## One Less. One More.

Watching your regrets go up in flames is a wonderful way to start the New Year feeling fresh and unburdened, although you certainly don't have to wait for a specific time of year to either physically or symbolically burn your regrets, those past events you no longer control, and let them go.

*When one door closes another door opens; but we so often look so long and so regretfully upon the closed door, that we do not see the ones which open for us.*
*– Alexander Graham Bell*

Remember, regrets are not real, although they feel that way. Like fear, regrets are only thoughts in your mind, feedback that the ego is trying to control something it can't. No held regret ever gets you closer to happiness. Once you commit to following your heart and being happy, you must also commit to gently and compassionately seeing yourself as whole and complete in this present moment, releasing *anything* to the contrary, and that includes *all* your regrets.

Welcome regrets as feedback, but don't consume them. It's important to acknowledge all the ego's feedback, including the illusions of regrets.

Go slowly, knowing regrets are just more signs along your life's path, another example of your heart's perfect feedback system, shepherding you through the transition required for the fulfillment of your dreams and desires.

Once you commit to following your heart, gently coax

any negativity from the shadows, including your regrets, and let them go, knowing you're instantly back on the road to life mastery.

Mary Lynne,* a married, professional woman in her late 60s, held many regrets about starting her spiritual path late in life.

"I feel like I've missed so much," she said. "I regret I didn't commit to my happiness earlier, as my life could have been so much better. I wonder how many people in the world are like me, kind of rambling through life, procrastinating happiness, allowing other people, work, and society to direct my path, then just letting things happen, instead of consciously choosing to be happy and change my life?"

Mary Lynne regretted that she had possibly squandered away her life, yet I encouraged her to look closely at that feedback and flip it, telling me, instead, how her life has been worthwhile. I also reminded her about the billions of people who came before her, including her ancestors and other family members, who lived in much harder times and never had the space or opportunity to follow their hearts, or pursue their dreams and desires.

Mary Lynne went on for over an hour, telling me about her beautiful daughter, her wonderful husband, the influence she's had in her parents' lives, the closeness in her family, the successful risks she took in business, along with her travels, friendships, and her proudest professional accomplishment: graduating, "just for fun," from a prestigious cooking school.

"I've got to let all this negative crap go," she said, "because it's clearly just wasting my time."

Choose fewer regrets.

# Intention

I often hear, "How can I change my life and achieve my heart's dreams and desires if I let go of control? My happiness isn't going to happen by magic. I have to stay on top of things. I have to make it happen."

You can't make love, passion or happiness "happen." Love, passion and happiness are not something you do; they are states of being, experiences and expressions of alignment to your heart's purpose. Everything in your life, both now and in the future, is a result of your *intentions*.

Originating either from the ego or heart, intentions are the seeds for every thought, emotion, belief and action, the intended result of what you plant now, in the moment. What blooms in your life is a direct result of your precise moment-to-moment intentions.

Understanding both existing and future intentions is vital to letting go of old, negative habits and behaviors, and effectively choosing more thoughts or actions that contribute to your feeling aligned with your heart's calling.

"What is my intention?" becomes one of the more significant questions you can ask, and the fulcrum for your transition from ego to heart.

What is the intention of my existence?

What is the intended result of my life?

What was my intention when I started the fight?

What is my intention from reading this book?

What is my intention when spending time with my children?

What is my intention when I gossip?

What is my intention when I skip practice?

What, in this moment, is the intention of my thoughts?

What is my intention when I become emotionally unavailable?

Asking the question, "What is my intention?" immediately brings you present, creating a pause, a space, between your thoughts, emotions, and the subsequent actions; allowing a moment to consciously observe if you are under ego's controlling influence, and to let it go, or, instead, truly following your heart, and embracing the experience.

Get in the habit of asking yourself, "What is my intention?"

"I want this person ahead of me to speed up!" What is my intention?

"My life is bullshit." What is my intention?

"I want my spouse to be happy." What is my intention?

"Don't hire that person; I don't like the way they look." What is my intention?

"I want to be an NFL referee." What is my intention?

"I want to be rich." What is my intention? "I'm moving away from here." What is my intention?

"I'm going to take another business trip." What is my intention?

"Let's invite the pastor for dinner." What is my intention?

"I will be well." What is my intention?

"I want to fit in." What is my intention?

"I will not allow my child to attend sleep away camp." What is my intention?

"I want to control my own destiny." What is my intention?

"I won't eat that." What is my intention?

"I want a smaller waist." What is my intention?

"I decided I really don't want to go to the party." What is my intention?

"I'm establishing a charity for girls without fathers." What is my intention?

Intention always comes before action. Becoming aware of your intentions allows a conscious transition from ego's control to the present moment experience of fulfilling your heart's purpose.

When starting a charity, is your intention to selflessly serve others, or trying to heal an old wound?

When choosing at the last minute to attend a business party, is your intention to be spontaneous and have fun, or are you afraid of your boss's reaction to your not showing up?

When waiting at the stage door to congratulate the star, is your intention because you admire their work, or because you want to enhance your image by posting a selfie on social media?

Intention is nothing more than a pointer, another internal form of feedback. Don't waste time making yourself feel bad when discovering how many of your intentions are egocentric and self-centered. That's perfectly normal. As you awaken, learn from your ego-based intentions and let them go, and instead, consciously pivot to more fulfilling, present moment intentions from your heart.

# The Club

Choosing to release control, come present and follow your heart qualifies you for membership in the most extraordinary, *inclusive* club of all time; a group of souls who, from the beginning of humanity, believed, like you, that they were born to fulfill their life's purpose and do what they love. This timeless club has no name, entrance fee, secret handshake, password, or code, and anyone can join, although surprisingly few do.

For years, you resisted following your heart. You hesitated, made excuses, even convinced yourself at times that this club, this path of happiness and success, was for others, but not you. No more.

In joining this group of other like-minded, or more precisely, like-hearted individuals, you will be surprised by how similar your experiences are to others who also took the leap. Soon you'll meet those who, like you, detached enough from their fear, insecurity, resistance and doubt, for the exquisite joy of changing their lives and following their heart.

Committing to fulfilling your life's purpose signals the universe you are ready to let go of being controlled and reactive, and instead, prepared for the shift to a heart-centered existence, and the conscious fulfillment of your dreams. Yet, be aware, this period of transition is thick with tests and trials, and is never easy. You, like everyone else, when first committing to following his or her heart, must endure a universal rite of passage, an often frightening period of transition.

Every religion, culture, tribe and society, understands the importance of letting go of the past, and ceremoniously entering a new phase of life, using the rites of passage to immortalize life's notable transitions.

From birth to death, we commemorate significant transitions, including baptism, circumcision, the first haircut, confirmation, bar and bat mitzvah, *Quinceañera* in Latin American cultures, the Sweet Sixteen party, the debutante ball, pledging a fraternity or sorority, Mormon missions, graduations, weddings, and, in the Marine Corp, recruits face the Crucible, the final, grueling fifty-four-hour test before officially becoming a Marine.

Now that you've made the conscious, committed decision to change your life, the transition you experience marks the beginning of your daily, lifelong process of *slowly* and incrementally letting go of everything that no longer aligns with your heart's calling, and, instead, experiencing more happiness and fulfillment than you've ever dreamed possible.

Think of yourself as a hot air balloon tethered to the earth, and then, at the given time, throwing off the ropes – the former you – lifting higher and higher, letting go of the restraints and resistance to gain new, grander perspectives on your heart-centered landscape.

*How many times during the day do you find yourself fighting against something, and very often it's yourself? If you surrendered to the air, you could ride it!*
— Toni Morrison

# Crabs in a Pail

I admire anyone who courageously faces his or her crisis, fears, addictions and follies. These intrepid souls, after dealing with their demons, and consciously committing to following their heart, are often surprised by the number of so-called friends, colleagues and even family, who inevitably try to pull them back into the same addictive, destructive behaviors, they just committed to let go and leave behind.

My fishmonger friend Colin Mather owns The Seafood Shop, an incredibly popular fish store in the Hamptons, on the eastern end of New York's Long Island. One afternoon, a local fisherman brought in a freshly caught bucket of beautiful Atlantic blue crabs, and watching them, I noticed that every time one crab tried to climb out of the bucket, the others reached up and pulled him back in.

"If you're going to follow your heart," Colin told me, "make sure you don't get caught in a pail with a bunch of other crabs."

Most people are initially disheartened when having to let go of their toxic relationships, finding it difficult saying goodbye to old friends and lifestyles, knowing, ultimately, they will only try pulling them back down. However, once they commit to letting go of their past and instead, embrace this time of transition, they, like you, walk out of the fire stronger, more empowered than ever.

Like a child discovering something new, you want to share your enthusiasm and fresh heart-felt wonder with the world. And yet, the world you've known, and the people in it, may not be ready for your boundless spirit. Nevertheless, press on, because just around the corner, the universe will deliver a whole new set of relationships and circumstances aligning perfectly with your unfolding new passionate adventure.

Let go of your need to be accepted by others, and simply experience your expanding happiness and purpose. As awareness and commitment to your life's purpose deepens, the trials will continue. You will lose relationships, although eventually gain new, higher conscious, friends. And, like all transitions, once you recognize that your internal strength is far greater than any external impediment, your heart-centered travels may occasionally be slowed, although never stopped again.

# Keep Going

You are changed. There's no doubt about it. You are a new person, connected to your heart, alive with potential, opportunity and excited by the future.

You are now on the inside, a card-carrying member of the club, ready for a new life filled with all its promises.

"Look out world, here I come!" you shout.

But wait, there's a problem. Inside, you're changed. Outside, to most everyone else, you still appear as the same person you were before.

Now, you're one month sober. To everyone else, you're still a drunk.

Now, you're the boss. To everyone else, you're still the junior executive.

Now, you're acting in your first movie. To everyone else, you're still the shy kid from around the block.

Now, you're rich. To everyone else, you're still the paperboy from the projects.

Now, you're in a committed, loving, mentally healthy relationship. To everyone else, you're still the high school player or floozy.

After all your hard work, all you've done, how far you've come, it would seem the world should recognize your efforts and welcome you with open arms. Unfortunately, nothing is further from the truth.

Matthew wrote in the New Testament (Matthew 13:57), "And they were deeply offended and refused to believe in him. Then Jesus told them, 'A prophet is honored everywhere except in his own hometown and among his own family.'"

You chose to follow your heart and awaken. Most everyone else around you, though, remains asleep.

Changing your life is a personal calling, not a collective mandate. Initially, not everyone shares your excitement, few will recognize your effort, and almost no one truly understands – nor can they – the depth of your awakened heart. Be aware that for many around you, your transition is a disheartening mirror, a sad reflection of their ego's discontent. Let it go.

Let go of trying to control other people's reaction to your journey, and instead, fill yourself with the possibilities created by your heart-directed intentions.

Are you starting a new business? How many people, families, industries, countries, organizations and more will be affected by your decision? Keep going.

Are you letting go of regrets? Anger? Fears? Remorse? Rage? Keep going.

Are you switching direction? Changing gears? Moving away from darkness toward light? Keep going.

Are you letting go of the blame game and taking responsibility? Are you choosing to lead instead of follow? Are you finally getting the help you need? Are you letting go of past hurts and coming present in gratitude? Keep going!

Are you laughing through the trials? Are you happy as you get well? Are you contributing to making the planet better than you found it? Keep going!

Trust this transition, and know you truly possess the strength, faith, vision, passion and fortitude to continue on.

Go slow. Be kind, compassionate and patient, recognizing that the outside world will take time accepting and appreciating your transition to the new you.

You will never completely know for sure how the universe – and all humanity – will change because of your bold and remarkable decision to follow your heart and discover your life's purpose, but be certain, that as you change, so will the world, and the people around you.

Joseph Campbell, the American mythologist, said, "When we quit thinking primarily about ourselves and our own self-preservation, we undergo a truly heroic transformation of consciousness."

Make no mistake, detaching from ego's control, and consciously choosing to follow your heart and do what you love is a huge deal.

It just takes time.

Take a deep breath and get ready. It's time to go all in.

# One Less. One More.
# Steps

1. Start now.
2. Come present.
3. Consciously choose to follow your heart, be happy and change slowly.
4. Today, choose one less controlling thought, or action, and let it go. One Less: Control.
5. Today, intentionally choose one more heart-centered experience.
   One More: Experience.
6. Celebrate your life's transition, and keep going!
7. Repeat tomorrow.

# Seven

## Raising the Stakes

**Less:** Hoping, Wishing and Trying
**More:** Doing

*I have been impressed with the urgency of doing.*
*Knowing is not enough; we must apply.*
*Being willing is not enough; we must do.*
*– Leonardo da Vinci*

**Traveling almost halfway around the world**, you fly deep into the heart of the jungle on a small single-engine plane, landing with a crash-like thud in a clearing on a tiny makeshift airstrip.

A muscular, indigenous guide, carrying a .416 Remington Magnum rifle, meets you in an open-roof, beat-up Jeep. Cautiously walking you along a muddy path through dense trees, you soon arrive at another clearing near a fresh water stream. Waiting for you, already prepared, is a sturdy, green, single person tent covered in mosquito netting, nestled adjacent to a burning fire.

Dropping your canvas travel bag to the ground, the

guide makes it clear that for the next several nights, you will be alone at the edge of the most dangerous part of the jungle. And, he says emphatically, if you value your life, do not even consider venturing more than a few hundred feet away from your base camp until the next set of guides arrive sometime in the following forty-eight hours.

This is it. You are trained, prepared and committed, for this twelve-day, one hundred-mile trek through the wild, remote and dangerous native bush.

You have about five more seconds to back out of this adventure, and although a fearful voice in your head screams, "Get me out of here!" you're not going anywhere.

You've worked your whole life for this very moment, which will culminate in a remarkable journey, and for you, there are now zero options for giving up.

You are resolute and about to raise the stakes.

Aware there is uncertainty and real danger ahead, and acknowledging your feelings of anxiety and concern in this new, unfamiliar and challenging environment, you still know, from the core of your existence, that because you consciously stopped wishing for adventure, and instead, chose to follow your heart, you have never been happier, or more excited to be alive.

With a concealed gulp, and no outward hesitation, you wave goodbye to your guide as he disappears back into the thick jungle. Unpacking your supplies, as the day's remaining light slowly fades and the jungle awakens, you prepare for this unrivaled expedition, knowing deep inside that you are on the threshold of something big.

# Less Hoping and Wishing

There's a wonderful, romantic, childlike quality to hoping and wishing.

You grew up wishing on stars, having three wishes, wishing in a well, coins in a fountain, blowing out birthday candles, and, as seeds scatter carelessly into the wind, making a wish while puffing at a dandelion.

Hope, too, carries the strong belief of a desired expectation, a sense if you hope strongly enough, an ideal result will appear.

On the surface, wishing for something to come true looks as though you are being positive and optimistic.

Yet by wishing and hoping, you suspend your heart's authority, reducing yourself to a separate, small, insignificant piece of humanity, and as the ego directs, having you cross your fingers in the hopes the universe will take notice and grant your request.

There is nothing wrong with hoping or wishing for something to happen, and certainly, feeling hopeful is more productive than desolation or doom. However, actually showing up, coming present and proactively working to produce change, dramatically improves your chances for success.

I say the Lord's Prayer, Matthew 6:9-13, every day and have for my adult life. I am struck by the directness and strength of the prayer's call to action, especially the verses, "Give us this day our daily bread," "Forgive us our debts," and, "Deliver us from evil."

There is no wishing or hoping here about the way Jesus directs his disciples to pray. His instructions are clear: *Set your intentions and don't ask; tell me what you want.*

Hoping for your life to change is passive, a thought the universe may – just may – possibly move in your favor.

Charles Revson, the creator of Revlon Cosmetics, said, "In the factory we make cosmetics; in the drugstore we sell hope."

Hoping for a positive outcome feels better than losing hope. Visit any casino and watch how the dealers, just like Mr. Revson, understand the power of giving gamblers a sense of hope. Yet, consider how many gamers leave winners? The entertainment industry, promising future rewards and fame, strings actors and writers along with hope, birthing the expression, "In show business you will die of encouragement."

Hoping and wishing subtly shifts the appearance of power to the ego and temporarily away from your heart. Preparing for the worst and hoping for the best is fine, yet, how does it feel when your wish or hope doesn't come true?

And, when hopes and wishes do come true, it only temporarily feels good. Digging deeper, the euphoria is really fear-based relief. Deep down you worry that, although this time you dodged a bullet, maybe the next time, despite your wishes and hopes, things won't end as well.

On TV, a news reporter standing knee deep in flood water in an American Midwestern town, commented on the devastation from torrential rains and overflowing river banks, saying, "As rivers reach historic levels, this community is at a loss to stop the rising water, and at this point residents can only *hope* for a miracle."

The reporter's vapid comments filled airtime, but, in fact, hundreds of townspeople weren't hoping for anything at all because they were already too busy taking action, helping their families, supporting their neighbors, laying sandbags along the banks and comforting and praying with others who also lost everything. The reporter got it wrong. This wasn't a story about hope; it was about heart-centered action.

Imagine this pilot's announcement just before taking off on a long flight, "Good evening, ladies and gentlemen, and welcome to Hope Air. We have a great crew, and we've spent a bunch of time hoping we will get you safely across the ocean. We *hope* nothing goes wrong, and *hopefully* we can land this thing at the right airport, and, like you, we hope our engines hold out, the wings stay on, and the plane sticks together, so we can hopefully get you down without any problems. Anyway, that's our wish, and we're hoping that everything goes right, so, like us here in the cockpit, go ahead and cross your fingers, say a little prayer and, God willing, nothing bad will happen! Thanks again for flying Hope Air, and we hope you enjoy your flight."

There are times I catch myself saying, "I hope . . ." When I'm waiting for someone at the train station, I *hope* his or her train is on time. I hope my team will win. And recently, when a college girl went missing, there was nothing more I could do but hope and pray for her safe return.

Yet, when it comes to following your heart, moving toward life mastery, and creating the world you've always dreamed of, as Dr. Benjamin Ola Akande, the dean of Webster University's Walker School of Business and Technology, said, "Hope is not a strategy."

## Franklyn Wilson's Back Pain

I worked for several years with Franklyn Wilson,* a highly respected CEO in the defense industry. A powerful and confident man, Franklyn suffered from chronic back pain. Although he occasionally took pain medication, tried different stretches and exercises, actively controlled his stress, maintained regular visits to chiropractors, and vigilantly scheduled regular medical examinations, there did not appear to be anything physically amiss to cause the acute pain.

Following Franklyn's promotion from running a North American division to heading the entire worldwide operation, the company's board of directors engaged me to help Franklyn build his personal brand as a global leader. When traveling together, we usually flew; however, on this trip we shared a long European train ride.

After discussing business, Franklyn, looking out the window to the snow-capped Alps, said, "I wish I could get rid of my back pain. I get excited, hoping my next treatment will work, until I realize I really don't know what to do, and I'm running out of options."

I asked Franklyn if he was willing to do something different.

"Sure, anything," he said.

I told him to imagine his backache was a business matter with a mathematical solution, and he had just three months to solve the issue. No excuses, no alternatives, fix the problem, period.

Also, as part of the assignment, I instructed Franklyn to do the One Less, One More math, meaning everyday he was to let go of one act of hoping or wishing, and, conversely, proactively completing one more action-oriented task toward becoming pain free.

"I get it!" Franklyn said, springing into action. "I'm going to focus on the solution, not the problem."

Within an hour, he had written an entire plan, complete with a goal, objectives, strategies, resources, charts and tactics, resulting in having no back pain within three months. Franklyn created a specific spreadsheet just to track the elimination of his hopes and wishes relating to his back pain, along with a separate column for daily results on his one less and one more activities. Further, Franklyn also noted patterns that contributed to the pain, possible unexplored solutions, including an inversion table, along with the exploration of several natural anti-inflammatory healthcare products.

Watching Franklyn in action made it clear why this young CEO graduated university at the top of his class, and rose to prominence in his company so quickly.

Two months after our train ride, Franklyn's back pain was almost completely gone. Through a combination of exercises to strengthen his core, no longer wearing his wallet in his back pocket, and several other personal changes, Franklyn Wilson went from wishing his back pain would disappear, to taking charge – something he did very well – and becoming pain free with the added bonus of improved posture and fitness.

When Franklyn switched from focusing on his problem, and merely hoping he would feel better, to concentrating on the desired result of a strong core, strong posture and no pain, he aligned with what made him feel good, and, with small-scale, practical and incremental effort, succeeded at something that had eluded him for years.

## Less Trying

Trying is an excuse to fail.

Trying is cloaked resistance, a commitment to the attempt, not the completion of an action. Trying, like wishing and hoping, is a subtle obstacle to fulfilling your heart's desire, because inherent in the attempt to pursue your passion, is also the growing seed of failure.

Once you choose to change your life, follow your heart and be happy, trying is no longer an option.

You must consciously choose less trying and more directed action toward your specific goals, dreams and desires.

Don't confuse persistence with trying, because they are vastly different.

Trying holds the underlying intention of being recognized for the effort, not the achievement. Persistence, though, is unrelenting trial and error that follows committing to, and actively engaging in, reaching a goal.

*I have not failed. I've just found 10,000 ways that won't work.*
*– Thomas Edison, responding to a question about his persistent*
*work related to discovering a sustainable storage battery*

Edison was steadfast in his belief that he would discover a solution, and his subsequent work was focused on the successful completion of his goal, not the myriad failed attempts.

Become conscious of the times you say, "try," and acknowledge your focus may be on the process, not the achievement of your goal.

# Drop the Pencil

Do this exercise:

Pick up a pencil or similar object and *try* dropping it.

I'll bet you dropped the pencil. Everyone does, at first.

The problem is I told you to *try* dropping the pencil, not to drop it.

Do it again.

Try dropping the pencil.

Did you drop it, or not?

If you dropped the pencil, you failed at following my direction because you completed an action. And, by trying and subsequently not dropping the pencil, how do you feel? Frustrated? Unfulfilled? Thwarted? Discouraged? That's because trying without the specific intent for accomplishment is emotionally unfulfilling.

Saying, "But, I tried!" is an excuse that *never* feels good.

However, failing to achieve a goal, if *persistently* pursued, is simply a step closer to fulfillment. Conversely, *trying* to achieve something is committing to the attempt, not the completion.

Do you get it?

Trying to drop the pencil is impossible, and it's the same in life.

Drop a pencil, or don't.

Open a pet day care, or don't.

Get a tattoo, or don't.

Build a new chapel, or don't.

Write a screenplay, or don't.

Surf, or don't.

Cut your hair, or don't.

Clear your cupboard of junk, or don't.

Lose weight, or don't.

Go to therapy, or don't.

Get over him, or don't.

Make love, or don't.

Become a chef, or don't.

Raise the money, or don't.

Go to Paris, or don't.

Play golf, or don't.

Do your homework, or don't.

Start over, or don't.

Become vegan, or don't.

If you fail, keep going, regroup, or stop. Either do it, or don't. But don't bother trying.

Release, "I'm trying," from your experience, and consciously switch your entire focus to actually accomplishing a goal, dream or desire.

Which feels more powerful and authentic?
I'll try not to gossip.
I don't gossip.

I'm trying to eat less gluten.
I'm slowly becoming gluten free.

I'll try not to be so critical.
I will not judge or be critical.

I'll try not to be so needy with my lover.
I am becoming a more attentive and giving lover.

I'll try not to cheat on my taxes.
I don't cheat on my taxes.

I'll try not to drink and drive.
I drive clean and sober, or I find someone else to drive.

I'll try not to flirt with married men/women.
I don't flirt with or date married men/women.

I'll try not to make decisions out of fear.
I monitor my emotions and make sound decisions.

I'll try not to procrastinate.

Starting tomorrow, I will be proactive  (Just kidding. Start now.)

I'll try not to treat family members with contempt.

I love my family and treat them with compassion and kindness.

I'll try not to yell at subordinates.

I respect my subordinates and treat them accordingly.

I'll try to exercise three times a week.

I exercise three times a week.

I'll try getting a new job.

I created a strategic plan for obtaining a new job. I take action every day toward finding a new job, and I will be employed within four weeks.

I'll try getting better grades.

I dedicate three hours a day to my studies, I go in early for academic support, and I balance my free time for physical activity and plenty of sleep. My goal is a B+ average.

I'll try to lose weight.

I joined a weight loss program and already lost twelve pounds. My goal weight is (blank), which I will achieve in (blank) weeks.

I'll try to start a new company.

I started and registered my new company. Along with my business partner, we're working on the business plan, and will be operational in seven weeks.

I'll try not to be so selfish.

I consider other people's feelings and share when I can. I ask my family and friends to remind me when I'm being selfish.

I'll try not to spend so much money.

I stick closely to my budget.

Once you decide to follow your heart, be happy and slowly change your life, it doesn't matter if you succeed or fail, just keep going. Consciously commit to more daily heart-centered actions, and less time wasted, hoping, wishing and trying.

## More Doing

*Nothing happens until something moves.*
*– Albert Einstein*

At conception, from the moment you moved from the invisible into an emerging body and eventual consciousness, all your actions, ultimately, originated from your heart's desire to experience and express your true nature. That hasn't changed then or now.

**One Less. One More.**

In every moment, you are given the opportunity to either resist or respond to your heart's longing, leaving you, whether conscious of your role or not, as the arbiter of the resulting action. Choosing inaction as a result of your heart's calling is still action.

All your actions begin with a thought, followed by an emotion – the reaction or feedback to the thought – which then, through either a conscious or unconscious choice, may or may not be followed by a resulting external or physical action. All action – and allow me to repeat – *all* action, results in some form of change.

Whether aware of it or not, every action is unique, with its own distinct beginning, middle and end. Although over time, it may appear that you are habitually repeating an action, no two actions are exactly alike, nor do they take place in identical circumstances. Every action is born fresh in either resistance or alignment with your heart's desire.

Further, you produce two forms of action: internal, which always come first, and then external, which come as a result of an internal action. It is possible to have an internal action without a subsequent external action; for example, when you catch yourself feeling angry and choose not to react. *All* external actions begin internally.

Every action is dominated by either a resistant ego-centered energy or heart-centered energy, yet no action is 100 percent pure. Even the most well-intentioned, heart-centered action contains some aspect of the ego, and the most self-centered, egocentric action, still contains expressions of the heart.

Until now, the majority of your actions have been unexamined, unintentional and mostly in reaction to something else. Become aware of the thought-emotion-action process, and deliberately, intentionally, choose and experience more heart-centered actions.

## Raising the Stakes

I asked my cousin, John Vorhaus, one of the leading poker experts in the world, to tell me about raising the stakes in both the game of poker and in life.

John told me, "Every poker player knows of something called "the gulp limit," that place in a poker game where the amount you wager makes you go *gulp*. For some people, their gulp limit is zero – they simply can't stand to bet. For others, their gulp limit has no limit – they can wager any amount and always feel good. For the rest of us, the gulp limit is a sliding scale: The more accustomed to risk we become, the higher our gulp limit goes. Raise the stakes and you raise the fear."

Are you all in? Are you experiencing fear and resistance because you're now fully in the game? Have you heroically taken action to follow your heart, and reached your gulp limit? Are you just a little terrified? Good. Now keep going.

Maybe your gulp limit is just reading this book and awakening to the possibility that you truly were born to be happy.

Possibly your gulp limit is choosing to trek the African bush or write the second chapter of your first children's book. Maybe your gulp limit is changing your diet to heal an illness, overcoming a lifelong fear, building muscle mass, becoming a Boy or Girl Scout leader, learning to play the flute, opening an organic café, speaking Japanese, or becoming a more present parent.

Maybe you've reached your gulp limit because you quit a management job to become a nurse, or, after working for someone else, you opened your own salon, or left your comfy day job to launch a new product.

Maybe you've reached your gulp limit because you just landed the biggest assignment of your career, a famous client just hired you, or you received the largest order of your life. Maybe you're at your gulp limit because, while others talked about it, you ran and won a city council post; were promoted from orchestra violinist to concertmaster; general manager to vice president; or U.S. Army Specialist to Sergeant.

Or just maybe you reached your gulp limit because, after years of incurring mind-numbing debt, you've cut up your credit cards, or this is your first day out of rehab. Maybe you were elected to the school board, came out, finally admitted to your siblings that your parents were right, or, perhaps had the courage to go into therapy, discovering that your parents were wrong.

*There are very few human beings who receive the truth, complete and staggering, by instant illumination. Most of them acquire it fragment by fragment.*
*– Anaïs Nin*

Right now, clarity and balance of your thoughts, emotions and actions is what you seek, although over time, your goal, of course, is to increase your heart-centered actions.

As you grow and expand in this new world, you will be challenged and tested in ways you cannot possibly imagine.

Although you're all in, committed to this journey, and begun talking the talk, the walk ahead still requires creative, practical, heart-centered action, great faith, and persistence.

Take it slow. Don't push it or do too much, too soon.

One less. One more.

Who do you know that boldly took action to follow their heart?

Who do you know that courageously changed their life and really did something to make a difference?

Who in your circle of relationships stepped out of their comfort zone to master their life, pursuing a truly unique path of happiness?

Who, at the continued risk of danger, fear and failure, still chose to take action, resulting in a better world?

Who do you know that proactively followed their passion to experience and express their own personal truth?

I'm betting one of those people is you.

On a deep level, raising the stakes and consciously initiating more heart-centered action feels like the right thing to do, it can also be frightening. Stay alert, because, although the ego insists there's nothing good or safe for you in this new, unchartered place, if you stay detached and carefully listen to both sides of the feedback, your heart will remind you that this is exactly where you need to be. Still, to experience your deepest passion, you have to believe and act on fulfilling your heart's purpose, and keep moving forward.

With every new heart-directed action, expect the feedback of fear and resistance. Listen as the ego says, "This is a problem, get me out of here," while your heart asserts, "Keep going. All is well."

As you choose less hoping, wishing and trying, and instead, proactively embark on more adventures, expect to initially feel off balance, apprehensive and uncomfortable for quite some time. Become vigilant in your observations, because, although the ego says you are entering a vastly strange and dangerous world, your heart knows in many ways, this is all surprisingly familiar, a homecoming of sorts.

This deeply emotional experience of internal conflict is the essence – the spirit – of all great stories throughout time. Ask anyone accomplished about experiencing fear while pursuing their heart's desires, and quickly discover your myriad similarities.

Recognizing the decision to follow your heart will probably be the hardest thing you'll ever do in this life. If you feel like a deer in the headlights, frozen with fear, with reservations about continuing on your heart's path, you are not alone. It is not uncommon after deciding to follow your heart that, along with fear, you also experience sadness, disorientation, remorse and confusion.

Be kind to yourself, take it slow, and allow your new life to evolve. You are never alone. And by intrepidly following your heart, you become the lighthouse on the cliff, the beacon of hope for countless others searching for light in their personal storm. Stay the course.

# Persistence

Right now, as you become aware of the dance between the ego and your heart, and consciously choose to try less and do more, there will be times you want to give up.

Regardless of previous accomplishments, or how successful and confident others may see you, or how committed you are to following your heart, once you're all in and reach your gulp limit, it is normal to tuck in your tail, feel like fleeing and quickly disappearing for home.

But you won't.

Don't quit now. Again, please: do not give up! All great follow-your-heart stories, including yours, are fraught with fear and uncertainty, and yet, the heroes persevere.

Harry Potter author, J.K Rowling, didn't quit after twenty-eight rejections and living on welfare. She turned a desperate life, filled with disappointment, into a billion dollar enterprise. Milton Hershey didn't quit, dropping out of the fourth grade and eventually starting three unsuccessful candy companies before founding The Hershey Company. American surfer, Bethany Hamilton, didn't quit after losing her arm to a shark attack, going on to inspire millions when she returned to professional surfing.

There are countless stories of people who refused to quit after facing extraordinary obstacles, internal resistance, fear, repeated failure, social pressures, unlimited obstructions, barriers, complications and disappointments. You, in your choice to follow your heart and be happy, are no different.

Hollywood can embellish details, but the soul of every story, including yours, is the heart's awakening, and the actions taken to express it. The ego resists heart-centered action; calling up every trick it knows to get your attention, which, of course, includes fear.

No worries. See ego's feedback, when following your heart, simply as information for the journey ahead, and then, every day, choose just a little less hoping, wishing and trying, and more heart-focused doing.

You raised the stakes just by choosing to follow your heart, and now, because you've not given up, it's time for your ultimate challenge.

# One Less. One More.
# Steps

1. Start now.
2. Come present.
3. Consciously choose to follow your heart, be happy and change slowly.
4. Today, choose to hope, wish or try one less time, and let it go. One Less: Hoping, wishing and trying.
5. Today, take at least one more action specifically focused on achieving a goal, dream or desire. One More: Doing.
6. You've raised the stakes, gone all in, and reached your gulp limit. Celebrate the game!
7. Repeat tomorrow.

**One Less. One More.**

# Eight

## Crisis – The Ultimate Challenge

**Less:** Blame
**More:** Accountability

> *Take your life in your own hands*
> *and what happens?*
> *A terrible thing: no one to blame.*
> *– Erica Jong*

**Nothing prepared me for** Reverend Buford T. Jones,\*
the business and spiritual leader of the popular New
Comings Evangelical Church.\*

Pastor Jones did nothing to hide his predilection for
elaborate mansions, private planes, fast cars, big money
and fancy clothes. What he had hidden from everyone,
including his wife and children, were several girlfriends,
a secret life of Internet pornography, and an offshore bank
account financed with embezzled church funds.

The New Comings church elders, a group of honorable
fundamentalist Christians, tried containing the developing
crisis, while convincing Pastor Jones to step down before

making a complete fool of himself and the church.

As events unfolded, Pastor Jones grumbled that this crisis was Satan's fault, an attempt to thwart his life-long efforts to build "a temple to the Lord that stood above all men."

As more individuals came forward with damaging evidence against Pastor Jones, and it became clear he could no longer lead from the pulpit, Pastor Jones's tone became more conciliatory. Still, he began blaming others for conspiring against him, saying certain people were jealous, angry and that some even wanted him dead.

"There are few men who walk this earth who want more for this church than I," Pastor Jones cried through tears, as his family and church leadership pleaded for his resignation.

As with most crises, and certainly those involving a person's reputation, events happen quickly, especially in this age of technology and instant communications. Although it appeared Pastor Jones had participated in this behavior for years, in just a matter of days everyone from law enforcement, the media, parishioners, bankers, insurance executives, community leaders and other national Christian leaders and organizations, knew every torrid detail of Pastor Jones's fall from grace, and it wasn't pretty watching him break under the pressure.

Covertly meeting at a motel about forty-five miles down the road from the church's headquarters, I told Pastor Jones, "You have a problem, a big problem, and if this church truly means something to you, you must do the right thing. Tell the truth, and step down."

Looking drawn and diminished, I reminded Pastor Jones that true leaders give all the credit and take the blame. I suggested he quickly reflect on how he would like this crisis to end for everyone involved, including his family, the church and community. I counseled Pastor Jones that he couldn't go backwards, and asked him to consider how, as the founder of the church, he wanted to be remembered. Although clichéd, I also asked him how he believed Jesus would handle this terrible situation.

Over the following difficult days, Pastor Jones acted as though the situation would go away. Church elders reluctantly began the process of legally removing him from church leadership, while others spoke anonymously to the press.

One night, during a tense, private, closed door meeting with Pastor Jones and the church board, a member of the leadership committee stepped forward and said, "Buford, this has gone on far enough. We're not leaving this room, and ain't no one going home until this situation is fixed."

Pastor Jones got up to leave, and a small, muscular man named Duke, stood up and said, "Reverend, I love you, brother, but with God as my witness, you're not going anywhere until you step down tonight."

At two in the morning, with Pastor Jones not budging, there was a soft knock on the door. No one moved. I answered the door, and standing in the dark hall was Bette Jones, Pastor Jones's wife of thirty-two years. A lovely woman with gentle grace, Mrs. Jones asked the elders and me to please give her and Pastor Jones the room. The church leadership went to their offices, and I waited in the church secretary's office down the hall.

Twenty-two minutes later I heard Mrs. Jones shut the door to her husband's office. She walked down the hall to where I was waiting, and calmly told me, "He's yours."

"And?" I asked.

"I told him: 'Own this, Buford, and do what these men say, or I leave you tonight.'" And with that, she turned and walked away.

Back in the room, Pastor Jones called the church leaders into his office, and together we successfully created a plan to ultimately bring this crisis to closure. Once Pastor Jones chose to follow his heart, and release his ego's feeble attempt to stay in control, he became accountable for his actions and the entire process moved swiftly. The following day, with no drama or blame, Pastor Jones delivered his final sermon, publicly admitting to adultery, fraud, misappropriation of funds, and what he called, "sins against my Father."

Today, several years later, Buford Jones is a changed man. He and Bette have repaired their marriage, and Mr. Jones is systematically paying back the $2.5 million he owes his church. After serving time in prison, he remains in intensive therapy for several forms of addiction, and spends hours volunteering at local churches and community organizations. Now peaceful and reflective, Mr. Jones slowly regained his reputation, while leading his church's efforts to build a satellite church in a neighboring town's low-income district.

"This crisis was the best thing that ever happened to me," Buford Jones said. "I was living a lie, and now that part of me died. Every day I spend less time thinking about me, and more time praising and serving the Lord. That's my one less and one more."

# Crisis

*Every little thing counts in a crisis.*
*– Jawaharlal Nehru*

To truly follow your heart, achieve your dreams and desires, to be free from life's perceived burdens, to awaken each morning more excited than the day before, to appreciate the life you've worked so hard to achieve, you must accept *every* crisis as an opportunity for personal growth and transformation.

Dealing with crisis is not easy, it never is.

Whether by choice or chance, you will experience myriad crises in your life. Crisis, on every level, both personally and professionally, is a tense, terrifying and frightening experience. The ego fights so hard to stay in control, and the heart so much wants you to let go.

The word crisis comes from the Greek, *krisis*, which means separation, a trial, contest, a decision for or against something.

Crisis, or the potential of a crisis, is an unexpected, non-routine event, producing a tangible and measurable break from normal, everyday reality, resulting in some form of conflict, test, or trial.

Crisis, whether mental, spiritual, physical, professional or emotional, disrupts goals, plans, schedules and projections for future events, creating havoc with the ego, which fears change. Regardless of any training or preparation, a true crisis usually comes with little to no warning, and until resolved, previous routines and coping mechanisms can no longer be maintained. Crisis always results in something ending, and the beginning of something new.

You can pray, call for help, hire a consultant, dial 911, or visit your therapist. At the end of the day, the nature or scope of your crisis is irrelevant. Nor does it matter who is to blame. A crisis, both large and small, is still a crisis, and demands your attention. What's important, though, is not that crisis happens to you. It will happen. What matters is how you handle crisis, and the choices you make *after* the crisis is over.

Crisis is an opportunity to revaluate and recalibrate your life, start fresh, follow your heart, and, ultimately, be happy. It's all your choice: Step through the door – the crisis – and become responsible for your life, or see yourself as a victim of circumstances, make excuses, blame someone or something else, feel bad and withdraw.

I know that is easier said than done.

In the mid-nineties, my friend and business leader, Scott Griffith, was diagnosed with stage II Hodgkin's lymphoma.

Scott told me, "I was in my mid-30s, in a steady relationship but not married, and like most guys my age, really focused on a professional track.

"I had been through business school and by all measures was having a pretty good career path, although I didn't have a mission, a purpose, to my life.

"After I received the cancer news, my brother Jerry told me, 'I know you'll fight this and survive. But, consider the kind of person you want to be when you're done with this experience. Think about coming out of this a different person than you go in.'

"I thought, *What's wrong with me now? Why do I need to be a different person when I'm done with this?*

"Still, what my brother said to me was this lightning rod moment. I remember writing it down, and it just started to sink in that life should be different after this. It forced me to develop a set of my own personal core values. I asked myself, *Do the people around me share my passions? My values?*

"I started questioning everything; the reason I joined clubs or what media I was watching or reading, and why. I started soul searching and decided to leave consulting.

"Then I thought, *What if I find a job that combines my passions for technology, game-changing business models, and sustainable urban environments – cities – and put that all together?*

"Soon after I was recruited to head the car sharing service, Zipcar.

"Many things changed since I kicked cancer, including now being happily married with a wonderful family, but this idea of following my heart and connecting passions to my career, is the reason I still pop out of bed every morning."

How do you handle crisis?

Do you seek the drama of crisis to appease the ego, or does just the thought of a crisis throw you into panic? Does crisis force you to relinquish control of your life's goals, and blame someone or something else for your apparent misfortune? When encountering crisis, do you go into hiding, hoping that eventually everything will go back to normal?

Or, do you use crisis as an opportunity to learn and grow? Does crisis help you become accountable for your life, follow your heart, and slowly, systematically, move more in the direction of your dreams and desires?

In crisis, choose between following the ego or your heart, because you can't choose both.

Moment by moment, day by day, as if torn between two lovers, you must choose whether your ego or your heart is the dominant driver of your life, embracing one, and cutting the other loose. This, for the rest of your life, will be your ultimate challenge.

Crisis produces a crack in your façade, revealing an underlying reality that requires a new set of choices. In crisis, you can either remain on the same path, with the same thoughts, fears and resistance you've experienced all your life, or detach yourself from this repetitive, negative cycle, and start from scratch based on your heart's calling.

You must choose between head or heart, because it is a physical, spiritual and emotional impossibility to walk two paths at the same time. You believed, prepared, committed and raised the stakes to fulfill your life's purpose. To truly change, be happy and follow your heart, you can no longer feign ignorance, create the noisy misdirection of inaction, or innocently wait for the stars to align in your favor.

Just as children grow and eventually become adults, the Apostle Paul wrote in 1 Corinthians 13:11, "When I was a child, I spoke as a child, I understood as a child, I thought as a child: but when I became a man, I put away childish things."

If you are to follow your heart, then you must herald the end of naïveté and take full responsibility for your life and the journey ahead.

You can't escape it: When you consciously choose to follow your heart, you must eventually say goodbye to your former ego-based self, and, ultimately, reemerge as the new you, the heart-centered person you were born to become.

Less blame. More accountability.

Which feels more authentic?

This marriage isn't working because of him/her.

If this marriage is going to survive, I need to work on myself first.

I was fired because my boss took advantage of my loyalty and never gave me a chance.

I was fired because I was more interested in pleasing my boss and playing office politics than doing my job.

I lie to protect everyone else.

## One Less. One More.

I will tell the truth and accept the consequences.

It's God's fault this happened.
I don't know why this happened, but I will use this terrible situation to make things better.

It's all his/her fault I lost fifty percent of my net worth. I never should have trusted that crook with my money.
I relinquished control of our finances and took my eye off the ball. In the future, I will take a more active role in all our financial decisions.

I don't have a problem, they do. I am a social drinker.
I am an alcoholic, I was powerless over alcohol, and I am now responsible.

She ruined my life.
I allowed things to get out of hand because I don't like conflict.

I failed the class because he's a terrible professor. Nobody likes him.
I didn't attend many classes, nor did I study, apply myself, or ask for help.

Being overweight is in my genes. I can't help it that I'm fat.
I take full responsibility for my well-being and choose to be fit.

The police are wrong. My wife hit me first, and I only spank my kids. I don't beat them like my parents hit me.

I'm in therapy to deal with my anger. It's true, I sometimes get so angry I want to hit my wife and children, but I've learned several ways to productively vent my rage, so I don't and won't use physical violence.

I cheated on my taxes because the government is corrupt.

I volunteer a significant portion of my time, and support political candidates, dedicated to tax reform.

# Dark Night of the Soul

*The nearer the dawn the darker the night.*
*– Henry Wadsworth Longfellow*

Becoming accountable, and taking responsibility for fulfilling your life's purpose, requires the confrontation of the demons, dragons and monsters you've elegantly avoided for so long. Now that you've chosen to follow your heart and do what you love . . .

What are you not confronting?

What fears keep you from moving forward?

What are you resisting?

What insecurity threatens you?

What truth are you not expressing?

What are you afraid is going to happen?

What is your major distraction?

What pain are you avoiding?

Why are you afraid to fail?

What's really bugging you?

What's keeping you awake?

What are you afraid is going to happen if you express emotion?

Crisis illuminates the clash between illusion and light, the fear-based ego and your love-based heart. Once you choose to follow your heart, change your life and be happy, the inevitable reality is you're going to have to face your greatest fears, and when you do, some aspect of your belief system, a part of who you thought you are, must die.

Carmelite monk, Saint John of the Cross, the sixteenth century Spanish Roman Catholic mystic, called this challenging time the, "Dark Night of the Soul." Mythologist, Joseph Campbell refers to this period, both in storytelling and life, as the "supreme ordeal."

Memorable movie characters in crisis often die symbolically before they can move on to achieve their ultimate goal, and you are no different.

In *Fight Club* (1999), Tyler Durden (Brad Pitt) said, "Only after disaster can you be resurrected. It is only after you've lost everything that you're free to do anything."

In *The Matrix* (1999), Neo (Keanu Reeves) dies at the hand of Agent Smith (Hugo Weaving) before being resurrected by Trinity's (Carrie-Anne Moss) love; and in James Cameron's, *Avatar* (2009), Jake (Sam Worthington) appears to die at the hands of the Na'vi.

Even in the adorable holiday movie, *Elf* (2003), before

Buddy (Will Ferrell) can connect with his true family, he must face death as he contemplates suicide while standing on the edge of New York City's 59th Street Bridge, a scene very similar to George Bailey's (Jimmy Stewart) attempted suicide jump from the Bedford Falls Bridge in Frank Capra's 1946 masterpiece, *It's a Wonderful Life.*

Jesus, experiencing his greatest mortal crisis, cried out on the cross, "Eli, Eli, lama sabachthani?" ("My God, my God, why have you forsaken me?")

During your time of crisis and transformation, expect to feel despair, scared, abandoned and alone, but you are not. Although this feels like one of the darkest points in your life – and it just may be – hold steady, and remember to slowly and consciously let go of anything that no longer fits in your life, and conversely, embrace those things you know align with your heart's path. Hang tough; take responsibility for your life, knowing deeply that you were born to follow your heart and be happy, and that eventually you will get through this intact, emerging stronger than ever before.

Every human being who chooses to pursue their dreams must at one time or another face his or her greatest fears, illusions, resistance and obstacles, and either continue on through the perils of self-realization, or quit and go home. Regardless of the ordeal, or how bad it looks now, like those who have navigated this water before you, I promise, if you persevere, you will emerge victorious.

# Like Them

*Be kind; for everyone you know is fighting a great battle.*
*– Philo of Alexandria*

Many people today are in real crisis.

You, like them, may be sick or in pain. Like them, you may be experiencing a financial crisis, your childhood still haunts you, or maybe you lost your job, flunked out of school, lost a loved one, or feel overwhelmed and depressed. Maybe someone disparaged you, or you slipped on the ice, or at seventy-five- or twenty-five-years-old, experience deep regret over mistakes you've made. Maybe you feel ashamed, insulted, suspicious, punished, manipulated, suffocated, powerless, teased, judged, unwanted, sad, lonely, anxious, dejected, upset, scared and worried. I get it.

Now, look around. Really, look closely at everyone around you. Even if you're alone, picture people in your building, at the mall, the folks that deliver your mail, or the staff that checked you into the hotel. Think about your family, relatives, ancestors, neighbors, co-workers and even people you don't like.

Every person around you on the ferry, in the gym, in the airplane, on the highway, in your office, at the concert, in the coffee shop, or on the street, share similar experiences to you. They all want to live longer and better, they want to be happy and understand the meaning of their lives. And they, like you, will experience numerous crises in their lives. And what will differentiate each person, including you, is not the actual crisis, but the way they deal with the crisis.

Dame Julie Andrews, at one time the world's most successful film star, lost her voice due to a botched throat operation, and never knowing if she would ever sing (or talk) again, followed her heart, persevered and, with great determination, returned to the stage, TV, film and writing. She went on to win a Kennedy Center Honors, a Grammy, Emmy, and a Screen Actors Guild Life Achievement Award.

In 1980, a drunk hit-and-run driver killed Candy Lightner's thirteen-year-old daughter, Cari. She went on to found MADD, Mothers Against Drunk Driving, one of the most successful grassroots campaigns ever.

In 1993, housewife and nurse, Carolyn Cook McCarthy's husband was killed by a mass murderer on New York's Long Island Railroad. In 1996, after launching a campaign against gun control, Mrs. McCarthy was elected to the United States Congress.

Ginger and Larry Katz lost their son, Ian, to a drug overdose, and founded The Courage to Speak Foundation®.

Best-selling author Stephen King was nearly killed when struck by a minivan along the side of a dark Maine road, and, after falling into a depression and nearly having his leg amputated, slowly returned to his prolific writing. Former South African president, Nelson Mandela, spent twenty-seven years in prison, and emerged full of love to lead the most peaceful transition of power in the world's history. Virtuoso violinist Itzhak Perlman contracted polio as a child, and became one of the world's most celebrated violinists. Dr. John Nash, the subject of the movie, *A Beautiful Mind*, suffered from paranoid schizophrenia, and went on to win the Nobel Prize. None of these people blamed their circumstances. Each of them became accountable for their personal experience, taking full responsibility for their futures, and slowly, with a tremendous amount of work and resolve, returned to their lives stronger than ever.

Although these stories are inspiring, they're not uncommon. For each one of these remarkable people, there are billions – yes, billions – of other people who consciously chose to use their crisis as a catalyst for positive change. You can, too.

What defines you, regardless of the intensity of the problem, tragedy, or suffering, is not the forces waged against you, but how you persevere and overcome these circumstances.

Regardless of your past, take full responsibility for your life today. Let the past fall away, and with a deep breath of confidence, trust your ego for feedback, follow your heart, and, using crisis as the catalyst for positive change, challenge *everything* standing between you and your passions, dreams and desires.

Consciously choose to believe that all is well.

# Less Blame and Excuses

*It's not whether you win or lose; it's how you place the blame.*
*– Oscar Wilde*

Self-realization is the hardest thing you will ever do. Yet, when you finally emerge from the cocoon of old patterns, false beliefs, fear-based decisions, phony relationships, insincere and shallow goals and desires, you emerge revitalized, exhilarated, victorious and forever changed.

So, what now? Run away or go deeper?

Energy healer, Irene Rebecca Bodendorf, counsels her clients when faced with a "dark night" experience to go deeper.

"Face it. Feel it," she says. "You chose to take this journey, connect with it."

There is no easy path around a transformative catharsis. Once you've answered your heart's calling, where is there to go? You've seen the light, and even if you run away, nothing changes until you release your fears and face your truth.

Are you keeping a secret?

Is there something you're afraid to admit?

What unfulfilled dream is calling you?

Do you hate yourself?

Are you afraid of what the doctor will tell you?

Is there somewhere else you would rather be?

Are you unfulfilled?

Broke?

In love with someone else?

Gay?

Are you not authentic?

This is your ultimate challenge, the opportunity to emerge victorious, and the best direction is straight in.

Choosing to follow your heart always sparks some form of personal crisis, where former systems fail, and what was normal, comfortable and safe, stops.

Although difficult at first to accept, what appears to be happening to you, is simply just happening, and what you choose – whether reacting from the ego or responding from the heart – is what, ultimately, determines the outcome. Every moment of your life is a lesson, a gift, or both. You choose.

I say this almost every day: It's *never* what happens to you; it's what you do with what happens to you that matters.

Cancer is not your enemy. Nor is a cheating spouse, a loss of fortune, a sick child, a car accident, addiction, or a missed opportunity.

You are neither too old nor too young, too late or too early. Your idea is neither good nor bad, and whether your efforts are recognized or not has no importance.

Your adversary is not the government, the director who rejected you for an acting role, the teacher who failed you, the boss who passed you over for a promotion, the friend who stopped talking to you, or the horse that threw you to the ground.

To truly master your life and achieve your dreams and desires, it's time to stop blaming your parents, God, fate, your weight, bad luck, your education, or whatever you believe are the reasons for your perceived failings. And, while you're at it, stop blaming yourself. It does you no good.

This is your test, and your test alone. To succeed, to do what you love, to walk forward into a glorious, exciting and rewarding future, you must stay put and remove the self-imposed obstacles and resistance in your path, knowing that you will eventually emerge victorious, conscious, enlightened, renewed and aware.

You do not need to face this crisis alone, but only you can walk across the burning coals.

Tolly Burkan, authority on the American fire walking ritual, and author of the book, *Dying to Live: A True Story of Life After Death*, told me, "I died to myself after my first fire walk. I was so unhappy with my life, miserable, really, that I had already twice attempted suicide. Deep in the California woods, the moment I first fire walked over 1,000+ degree hot coals, my limited and shallow belief system just died, and I was immediately reborn into a new person with limitless potential and opportunity."

Who do you blame for the problems of the world? Who do you blame for the violence, filth, poverty, pollution, addictions, and the myriad other problems we are assaulted with daily?

Do you blame yourself, the government, your spouse, children, parents, school, bosses, the weather, your neighbor's dog and everyone else, for your unhappiness?

Well, stop it.

Does an ounce of blame change anything? Never. Like a magician's sleight of hand, blame is smoke and mirrors, an illusion distracting you into believing that an external object is the cause of your trouble, so not to see where reality is really happening, which, as always, is at the center of your core.

Do you want violence to stop? Take responsibility and stop yelling, hitting, watching brutal media, playing vicious video games and acting out in rage.

Do you want an end to pollution? Take responsibility and stop littering. Find a better way to dispose of your waste, and stop using harmful chemicals in your home and on your lawn and garden.

Do you want your children to have a better education? Take responsibility and spend less time at work, on the computer, or talking to friends, and spend more time with your kids at home and school.

Do you want a more productive government? Take responsibility and understand the constitution. Learn about the roles each political leader plays, including the president, the governor, congressional, state and local leaders, and in every legal way possible, personally hold them accountable, reminding these elected officials they work for you.

Choose less blame.

# More Accountability

*Be the change you want to see in the world.*
*– Mahatma Gandhi*

Debbie* is a remarkable American chef and restaurateur. Growing up in the Pacific Northwest, she loved working in her father's organic vegetable garden, and as a teenager, found a job at a neighborhood natural food café. While other kids were off at dances and football games, Debbie spent countless happy hours at the café, prepping food, cleaning tables, and taking reservations. In her spare time, she developed unique raw and vegan food recipes and smoothies, which eventually became her trademark specialties.

Following high school, Debbie landed a spot at one of the world's top cooking schools, The Culinary Institute of America (CIA), in Hyde Park, NY. After graduating, she combined wanderlust with her passion for food, spending the next ten years working in prominent farm-to-table kitchens in Buenos Aires, Argentina; San Sebastián, Spain; Lyon, France; Sydney, Australia; and California's Napa Valley. Today, Debbie owns and operates several fabulous restaurants.

Debbie is a walking enigma. She smokes, drinks copious amounts of strong, dark coffee and diet soda, yet doesn't drink alcohol, and eats only organic food. She is known for her raw food prowess, yet to the horror of her many vegetarian friends and colleagues, loves organic, locally sourced meats, the gamier the better.

When several customers attending a national conference became ill from what appeared to be food poisoning after eating raw oysters at one of her restaurants, Debbie asked for my help.

The crisis grew quickly. The state and local health department wanted answers, and so did we.

The local media didn't yet have the story, but it was only a matter of time. Debbie wanted to control the story by calling a local TV anchor friend, although, as I counseled, that was not a good idea. Debbie's attorneys encouraged a blanket "no comment" press release statement, which was also not a good idea. The growing tension was palpable. As Debbie's executive chef worked with the shellfish supplier to source the oysters, her general manager handled the health department's requests for paperwork, while others conducted extensive inspections of every inch of her large, open and exposed kitchen.

That day, as the time neared for her restaurant to open, Debbie became more agitated. She began chain smoking unfiltered cigarettes, drank cup after cup of black coffee, and popped a few over-the-counter pills for her migraine headache. Then something terrible happened.

Debbie stood up, her eyes rolled back in her head, and she fell forward. Without making a sound, like a clothing store mannequin blown over by the wind, Debbie fell straight to the ground. With a grotesque thud, Debbie's face broke her fall.

For those of us watching her collapse, we stood frozen, certain she was dead. In a second, Debbie opened her eyes and groaned, snapping us all back into action. Luckily, Debbie's sous-chef, a volunteer emergency medical technician, quickly stabilized her until the ambulance arrived.

After a complete battery of tests and an overnight stay at the hospital, Debbie returned to work with a broken nose and a clean bill of health. The additional good news was that her customers, along with many other conference attendees, suffered from a virulent twenty-four-hour stomach flu. Their illness had nothing to do with oysters or any of Debbie's food.

Although relieved, Debbie was clearly in a funk.

"I nearly killed myself yesterday," she said, her broken nose covered with a splint and tape. "I got so worried, I just lost control."

Debbie reached for a hug, and trying not to sound judgmental, I whispered, "You've got a bigger problem."

Debbie pulled away, tensing at first in defense, and then relaxing just a bit to hear what I had to say.

"Tell me," I said, "if you're such a stickler for natural, organic foods, why, dear Debbie, do you refuse to exercise, while polluting your body with cigarettes, excessive amounts of coffee and diet soda?"

Pausing for a few contemplative moments, Debbie blurted, "I can't stop. I am so uncomfortable in my own skin, and my smoking and caffeine allow me an acceptable distraction to focus on something other than my unhappiness. I want to quit, I just don't know where to start."

Finally, opening her heart and taking responsibility for her own well-being, I asked Debbie, "As a teenager, when all your friends were out getting into trouble, what brought you to helping your father in his garden and eventually to the back door of that local health food café?"

"I love natural, alive, whole foods," Debbie said,

speaking with such passion I thought she was going to cry. "I love that unprocessed foods carry the energy of the sun into our bodies. I love knowing my customers are eating locally sourced, healthy, pure foods prepared with love and intention. I love the foodies in my industry, from the chefs to the farmers, my servers to the critics. I marvel that we cannot create new foods, only new ways to prepare those foods. And I am honored that my customers give me the opportunity to nourish them, and pay me, too!"

"How do you feel right now?" I asked.

"Warm and wonderful," she said.

I told Debbie to close her eyes.

"Now, think of an ashtray filled with spent cigarettes," I said. "How does your body feel now?"

"Disgusting," she said.

"Stop right there," I told Debbie. "Every day, just once before you light up, remember this disgusting feeling, and consciously choose not to smoke that one cigarette. See how long you continue smoking. That's your one less.

"Now, think of your organic garden in the sun," I said. "How does your body feel now?"

"Alive, amazing, magical!" Debbie said with a huge smile. "It's my favorite place in the world!"

"Good. Now make sure you give yourself the space every day to do or think of something in or related to your garden," I said. "Feel the experience, take note of what you discover, what inspires you, and how you can use your good feelings to create new dishes, improve your restaurants, and continue fulfilling your heart's purpose.

That's your one more."

Debbie hadn't built her business or reputation overnight. Her bad habits and underlying reasons for her self-destructive behavior weren't going away quickly, either.

"Take it slow," I said, "and every day focus on what brings you the greatest pleasure. At the same time, if something doesn't feel good, don't do it."

Debbie used her crisis as a catalyst for change. She slowly allowed herself to remove those aspects of her life that didn't feel good, which conversely, gave her more passion to truly follow her heart.

Admittedly happier than at any other time in her life, Debbie is now nicotine- and diet soda-free. She drinks an occasional espresso, and sees a mental health therapist twice a month, jogs and practices yoga. Debbie also works out with a trainer, and recently joined a spiritually centered community near her home. As Debbie's other restaurants thrive, she is opening her first vegetarian restaurant, writing a farm-to-table cookbook, and for the first time since I've known Debbie, has a compassionate and loving partner.

In all great stories, the challenge of choosing between the head and heart will always be the hero's definitive crisis. For you it's no different.

Step through the fire of your heart's purification, and emerge stronger, clearer and with a greater sense of purpose than ever before.

This is your moment of truth. This is where you put up, or shut up.

No more excuses, no more blame.

Say goodbye to old beliefs, fears, self-hatred, negative emotions, and myriad obstacles you've held dear for too long. This is the end to living a lie; a life lived according to everyone else's rules and regulations. To proceed on your heart's path, the ego's projection of yourself as a victim must perish, or at the very least, slowly fade away.

You alone need to fight this battle, face the monsters, triumph over your fears and resistance, vindicate yourself before the jury, win the prize, pass the test, emerge from the cave, survive the flames, slay the dragon, earn the maiden's hand, and prevail against all odds. This is your life; own it.

Pogo, the cartoon character by Walt Kelly said, "We have met the enemy, and he is us."

Come present and face your most formidable opponent, which, if you haven't already discovered, is really yourself. Consciously choose less blame for the perceived conditions in your life, and instead, become more accountable for following your heart and being happy.

Once you take responsibility for your life, and emerge intact from a crisis, the resulting breakthrough will change your life forever.

# One Less. One More.
# Steps

1. Start now.
2. Come present.
3. Consciously choose to follow your heart, be happy and change slowly.
4. Today, choose one less thought or action of blame, and let it go. One Less: Blame.
5. Today, take responsibility for one more aspect of your life, and embrace it. One More: Accountability.
6. Celebrate.
7. Repeat tomorrow.

## One Less. One More.

# Nine

## Choice

**Less:** Worse
**More:** Better

*But choose wisely,*
*for while the true Grail will bring you life,*
*the false Grail will take it from you.*
*– Grail Knight*, Indiana Jones
and the Last Crusade (1989)

*In the beginner's mind there are many possibilities;*
*in the expert's mind there are few.*
*– Shunryu Suzuki*

**Callie,\* an award-winning**, respected television executive, somewhere along her career, forgot to fall in love and get married, leaving her rich, powerful, single and childless.

Still, she wanted a family, so in typical Callie fashion, she skipped over finding a partner and went right to adopting Mei-Xing,\* a beautiful Chinese baby girl. From the moment Mei-Xing came home, Callie began making more conscious lifestyle choices.

Callie immediately quit smoking. "It's not good for me, it's not good for my girl."

Callie slowed her drinking to an occasional glass of wine. "What good is raising an angel if you're too drunk to enjoy her?"

Callie cleaned her cupboards of junk and switched to organic foods. Baby-proofing her large home, she switched to natural, non-toxic cleaning products, and installed a built-in water filtration system.

"I want a healthy home for Mei-Xing as she grows up," Callie said.

One night over dinner at Spago in Beverly Hills, Callie and I discussed our children and academic research indicating a possible link to increased hostility among teenagers playing long hours of violent video games.

"It's good what you're doing at home for Mei-Xing," I said to Callie. "Can you do the same in your business?"

"Of course," Callie said, emphatically.

"Then why," I asked, "do you produce TV shows and movies with so much gratuitous sex, graphic violence and dark themes?"

Without missing a beat, Callie went into her First Amendment spiel about, "I'm-only-giving-people-what-they-want-and-they-don't-have-to-watch-it." She wasn't angry or defensive, just on autopilot, and we dropped it there.

After a wonderful evening, Callie left without dessert

or after-dinner drinks, getting home in time for Mei-Xing's bedtime routine.

I returned to New York, and a few days later received a call.

"What do I do?" Callie asked frantically. "I had this revelation, and feel like I just woke from a bad dream."

Callie explained that during a development meeting, several young executives were pitching new story ideas, and without thinking, she began silently asking herself, "How will this contribute to Mei-Xing's life? Do I want my daughter and her friends watching this TV show when she grows up? Are the shows we're producing making our children's lives better or worse?"

Callie was shaken by her Aha! moment.

"Relax," I said. "You're simply becoming conscious, and it's all good. Stay present and keep monitoring your feelings. Listen to what your feedback system is telling you."

Callie's experience is common for people in power, especially for new parents with shifting perspectives. I suggested for the next couple of weeks Callie do nothing but observe her team, and, using both her heart and head as feedback, slow down projects that don't fit with her new sensitivity, and, conversely, when a new concept comes in that feels more intuitively aligned to her new perspective, she consider trusting her instincts and *green light* the pilot. One less. One more.

I spoke to Callie several months later.

"My new point of view is, 'for better or worse,'" Callie

said. "I can't change Hollywood, but I can become more conscious of my responsibility in the industry, and how my choices are either contributing to our culture or not. If we can produce profitable entertainment product with fewer sinister or tasteless themes, and without preaching, shine just a little more goodness and light through the screen, I'm doing okay for my girl and me."

In every waking moment, you have many choices. In this moment, right now, what choice will you make?

Left or right?

Up or down?

Help or hinder?

Fight to be right, or compromise for a joint solution?

Speak harshly or compassionately?

Contribute or not?

Medicate or meditate?

Go in or walk out?

Have children or not?

Give in or give up?

Criticize or commend?

Complain or praise?

Fight or flight?

Proceed or stop?

Yes or no?

Truth or lie?

Better or worse?

Consciously knowing what you want from life narrows

all your choices; either you're aligned to your heart's desire, or you're not. There are, however, few absolute choices. For the most part, you either negate your heart and pursue the ego, or follow your heart, and relegate the ego to a useful feedback mechanism. Conscious choice requires you to become present, ultimately choosing between the voice in your head, or the calling of your heart.

The universe is infinite, as are the incalculable opportunities available for fulfilling your dreams and desires. Learn to question your choices, to trust your emotional feedback system, and benchmark your feelings against your intention to follow your heart and be happy. Although the ego is impatient, your heart is infinite, and in no hurry. Reflect on your choices, and when stumped, question whether your choices will result in making life better or worse. Trust your heart, and the answer will always become clear.

*Make me an instrument of thy peace.*
*– Saint Francis of Assisi*

In every conscious moment, what will you choose? Ultimately, there is only one choice: Will you make this moment better or worse?

As you awaken to a life lived more from the heart than head, your reality takes on a new quality, a texture unlike anything you've ever experienced. You are moving toward mastery, foiled less by the resistance of fears and negative emotions, and more by the joy and peace of a fulfilled heart, alive and on purpose. And with this awakening comes knowledge. And with this knowledge comes choice. And with these choices come action. And these actions – every action – result in consequences that profoundly change the world, either for better or worse. Remind yourself at every opportunity, "Will my choices in this moment result in making the next moment, and subsequent moments, better or worse?"

By choosing to follow your heart and be happy, you also accept responsibility for living fully in the present moment, the only moment there is. What you choose in this moment influences the next moment, setting in motion thought, emotions, actions and consequences, ultimately, creating quantifiable events perceived by others as reality. Everything in and around your life is a product of choice. Every current choice holds profound influence later.

Your birth granted you the keys to life's castle. How will you rule the kingdom?

*We are made wise not by the recollection of our past, but by the responsibility for our future.*
*– George Bernard Shaw*

Where are you in this moment? What are you thinking now? Do your thoughts move you in the direction of making this and the next moment better or worse?

Are your current actions negative, fear-based, ego-filled and resistant to your heart's journey? If so, then, by the laws of nature, your subsequent actions will not – cannot

– align with your goals, dreams and desires. Choose less resistant, fear-based and negatively influenced thoughts that eventually will produce resistant, fear-based and negatively influenced actions.

Conversely, if your current thoughts are heart-centered, affirming, compassionate, encouraging, filled with enthusiasm and passion, then, by the laws of nature, your subsequent actions will result in the same. It may sound terribly simplistic, but when you catch yourself thinking negative thoughts, use that feedback and consciously switch to more positive, happy, productive thoughts. This simple switch from negative to positive thoughts *always* results in a constructive outcome.

And even when things don't go your way, as they often don't, you can still consciously choose to make each situation better purely by releasing negativity and resistance, and intentionally infusing the current moment with more of your heart's love and light.

You are maturing in your role as a creator, a life master, and, much like the superhero who begins comprehending his or her own newly discovered powers, you, too, must choose whether to use your gifts, your ability to influence the future, for better or worse.

## Less Worse. More Better.

In the early 1960s, while studying the science of chaos, late MIT mathematician and meteorologist, Dr. Edward Norton Lorenz, noted that small changes in a present condition might produce massive, large-scale changes in the future, calling this, "The Butterfly Effect." Dr. Lorenz demonstrated how theoretically the flapping of a butterfly's wings in Brazil, could imperceptibly change atmospheric conditions enough to possibly create a chain of events leading to a devastating tornado in Texas. So, here's the real question: Regardless of scale, grand decision or small choice, in every conscious moment, will you choose to make the universe, and the world around you, better or worse?

Ask yourself:

Will this choice make the present moment better or worse?

Will this choice strengthen or harm my relationship?

Will what I choose to ingest promote or diminish my well-being?

Will this choice support the planet or harm it?

Will this choice embrace or resist my heart's dreams, goals and desires, or not?

Will this choice contribute to making my finances better or worse?

Will this choice help me get better grades or not?

Will this choice encourage fear or courage?

Will my driving make the road around me safer or more dangerous?

Will this choice create calm or become a disruptive influence?

Will this choice negatively or positively influence my legacy and reputation?

Although no one sees me, if discovered, will this choice

benefit or jeopardize my reputation?

Will this choice raise or lower my children's spirit?

Will I choose to trash this rental car, hotel room, airplane seat, or restaurant bathroom, knowing someone else will clean up after me, or will I consciously choose to make the space better than I found it?

Will I choose to leave my friends feeling good, or will I sap their energy by gossiping, criticizing and complaining?

Is this prayer a veiled call for revenge or genuine gratitude for peace and reconciliation?

Is this choice a solution to the problem or an easy way out?

*Excellence is not a singular act, but a habit. You are what you repeatedly do.*
– Shaquille O'Neal

At least once today, consciously choose less chronic thoughts or actions making the next moment worse, and instead, intentionally, positively, influence the future by choosing more heart-centered constructive thoughts and actions.

*What do you repeatedly eat? What do you repeatedly say? What do you repeatedly think? What do you repeatedly believe?*

Consciously choosing to make this moment better, regardless of how many times you haven't in the past, breaks a negative cycle, and immediately starts creating a new, brighter future. This moment – right now – is the exact moment in time where your past ends and your future begins. *All* your power is right here in this present moment. Regardless of the past, by now choosing a thought or action from your heart, absolutely everything in the following moments change for the better.

Buddha said, "Words have the power to destroy or heal. When words are true and kind, they can change the world."

How do you talk to others? How do you talk to yourself?

How many times a day do you judge, criticize, gossip, complain, or accuse others with no basis in anything but negativity?

When was the last time you checked your tone? Are you harsh or loving? Is what you are saying straight and honest, or is your voice filled with anger, cynicism and resentment?

When our daughter, Molly, was a student at Convent of the Sacred Heart in New York City, one of her favorite teachers said, "Unless you have something kind, positive or helpful to say, don't say it." Sound advice for creating better moments. Become conscious of your approach to a problem, and learn a kind, constructive and compassionate approach to the solution, both for yourself and others. You create the future. Are you consciously making this present moment better or worse? Choose wisely.

## Breaking Through

Leon,* a married client with enormous influence, tried

unsuccessfully for years to stop womanizing. Despite countless hours of therapy, prescription drugs, forced separation from his family, support groups, and spirituality, his sex addiction continued.

Waking naked one morning, 4,500 miles from home, next to a woman he didn't know, Leon experienced a dramatic breakthrough. Getting out of bed at dawn, and, after years of deep soul-searching work, he sat staring out the window, and just as the sun broke the horizon, in that instant, he fully understood his overwhelming feelings of inadequacies and profound rage for his philandering, dead father. In the middle of another irresponsible and potentially dangerous sexual dalliance, Leon instantly recognized he must consciously forgive his father's infidelities and weakness, while taking full responsibility for his own life, marriage and success.

Leon heard himself say out loud, "Aha! This is it, I've gone far enough," and chose in that moment to begin living a new heart-centered reality of recovery and reconciliation with his wife, family, friends and, more essentially, himself. To this day, he has not wavered.

Breakthroughs are exactly that: The breaking through of internal resistance, including physical, mental, emotional, belief systems, fears and more. Breakthroughs are the visceral bond between your inner and outer worlds, the moment your heart eloquently aligns with your life's purpose. With no resistance, breakthroughs are the seamless symmetry between your heart, soul, mind and body, leaving you feeling excited, curious, connected and full of expectation. Breakthroughs provide clarity, becoming the benchmark for future decisions that result in making each moment better or worse.

Incomprehensible in scope, breakthroughs create new vistas and unique points-of-view, expanding your consciousness into higher realms, connecting you to even nobler insight and direction.

The world around you doesn't automatically change because you experienced a crisis and subsequent breakthrough, but when life returns to normal, nothing looks the same again.

A breakthrough may reveal the solution to a large piece of the puzzle. A breakthrough may reveal you are truly in love (or not). You may discover during a breakthrough that you can heal yourself, speak another language, drive a stick shift, ask for what pleases you, run a marathon, raise cattle, dance, influence school policy, break a habitual cycle, change direction, become more authentic, or experience something you never realized existed before.

You chose to follow your heart, committed to the process, determinedly showed up, did the required work and, without warning, the universe in its perfect timing, produced an unmistakable breakthrough, an opening to a higher level of consciousness. These are the "Aha!" moments.

Supporting your courageous decision to change your life and be happy, breakthroughs are, ultimately, divine gifts. In breakthrough moments, and possibly for the first time in your life, when the universe's traffic signal turns from red to green, and without the resistance of thought and ego, you instantly awaken to a new world with countless fresh opportunities and choices. Once your consciousness expands, there's no turning back.

*A single event can awaken within us a stranger totally unknown to us. To live is to be slowly born.*
– *Antoine de Saint-Exupéry*

Different cultures and practices describe similar breakthroughs as transcendence, satori, kenshō, bodhi, Buddhahood, prajna, illumination, Christ Consciousness or clarity of vision; all helpful descriptions if you're new to the journey.

Yet trying to predict or define breakthroughs is an exercise in futility. At the end of the day, no breakthrough will ever be anything more than a vivid moment on an eternal journey. And just as the word "relief" cannot begin to describe the experience of jumping into a cool, clear stream on a hot day, nothing can prepare you for a breakthrough moment of alignment and truth.

Consider the word enlightenment: *in light.* For just a moment, your vision after a breakthrough is illuminated, clear and bright, and although the actual breakthrough experience is fleeting, the awakening to an aspect of your own personal truth is eternal. More than likely you will never forget a breakthrough moment, that moment you realize you are exactly where you need to be.

Sophie,* a wonderfully talented American recording artist told me she experienced one of her most profound breakthrough moments when she heard her name called from the stage of LA's Staples Center to collect her Grammy Award. Even before she got out of her seat, Sophie instantly understood why her parents had been so insistent about her practicing piano every day after school.

"In that moment," Sophie said, "even though the crowd was cheering and I was physically moving toward the stage, time stood still, and I was flashing back over my life seeing that every single decision, choice, and compromise I made to follow my heart and pursue my music had now come together in a brilliant light of awareness. On a level far beyond thought and reasoning, I understood the profound and seamless connection between my life, my family, my music, fans and the stories I tell. All in that moment, I knew why I am here, and the choices I must make for my work ahead."

*Imagine a fertilized chicken embryo taking exactly twenty-one days to incubate, and finally after weeks in the dark of incredible internal growth, the hatchling breaks through its shell, entering a new, bright, and expanded world, and never able to ever go back inside again. This is you after a breakthrough.*

*After enlightenment, the laundry.*
*– Zen Proverb*

After a breakthrough, the world and the people around you are all the same, acting and reacting as they did before. Your boss is still an ogre, your lover insensitive, your neighbor seemingly out of control, and your finances still tipping in the wrong direction. You still have to take out the garbage, carpool for two hours to work, or sit for long evenings comforting an elderly loved one in a nursing home.

Your soul mate may never return, nor your eyesight, a limb, or the chance to bid on the 1954 red pickup truck you've been eyeing for the past ten years. And despite all your good intentions, your sister is still going to marry that jerk.

After a breakthrough, though, what is different is *you*.

It is not uncommon to hope that after a breakthrough life will be easier, all the pieces will fit, and your existential questions will be magically answered. In reality, though, once the first blush of the Aha! experience passes, you are often left with more questions than answers, realizing there is still so much more to do.

*Breakthrough moments aren't the end of the line; they are the beginning of a new chapter, with an entirely new set of choices. Ignorance is not bliss, and once you achieve the insight of a breakthrough, your choices become fewer and more apparent.*

Up until now, choosing to slowly and incrementally change your life, follow your heart and be happy, may have seemed scary and uncertain. Yet, in an instant of awakening, you break through the bonds of fear, resistance and ego, as the universe joyfully accommodates your heart's intentions, swinging open the gate to a glorious new reality.

After a breakthrough, you're automatically on the other side of resistance; knowing – really knowing – "I can do this!"

One fall morning after saying prayers, I walked into our living room and glanced outside at raindrops pooling on a lovely Japanese maple tree. For some reason, I was drawn to one rust red leaf as I watched the rainwater bead and then fall, bead and fall, bead and fall, as if in slow motion. And then, with no warning, I began seeing repeated mathematical patterns with indescribable beauty and clarity, an event I noticed happening on every leaf.

Although I still can't fully articulate the experience, in that astonishing luminous moment, I was observing an example of the universe's power and perfection, along with the absolute knowing that everything – yes, everything – is exactly as it should be, and that all is well. Even today as I write this, I can see – no, actually feel – that moment of beautiful truth and peace, which vibrationally now resonates through these words to you.

Breakthroughs are mind-blowing experiences, shattering illusion and resistance into golden fragments of eternal truth. Once you experience a breakthrough, your consciousness expands beyond the boundaries of the ego's limitations, extending your authenticity into a new dominion of awareness.

Lori* fulfilled her lifelong dream of owning a small, intimate, classic bookshop. After following her heart, quitting her job, and spending all her savings to open the bookstore, she experienced the greatest professional crisis of her life when a big national book chain opened down the street. Lori had to fight to stay in business and keep her customers, yet because of her persistent efforts, both online and within her local community, an influential magazine named her one of America's best booksellers, creating instant pride within her loyal customer and social media base, which, ultimately, resulted in increased customer traffic and a return to sustained profitability.

One cold winter's night, when Lori was closing her shop, a breeze blew off the street through the front display windows, ringing the small, antique brass bell hanging over the front door. In what Lori describes as, "A heavenly breakthrough moment," she stopped and slowly looked around her dark, empty, bookstore.

"I saw my shop as never before," Lori told me. "I knew in that moment everything happened perfectly – exactly as it should and on every level – and because I was following my heart, my little book shop would continue thriving."

After a breakthrough, your reality shifts forever; and what happens next in your life is all a matter of choice.

## Entitlement

After his multiple extra marital affairs, golf champion Tiger Woods admitted, "I thought I could get away with whatever I wanted to. You know, like entitled."

Catch yourself when feeling entitled and choose less of it, because no one owes you anything.

You are not entitled to respect, food on the table, fidelity, loyalty, good health, or a break. You are not entitled to a well paying job just because you graduated from college. You are not entitled to your children's respect just because you raised them. You are not entitled to your fair share, good service, or preferential treatment just because you are famous. As a consequence for agreeing to show up in this lifetime, your birthright is the capacity to experience and express your own personal truth. That's it. You are entitled to nothing more. If you want to follow your heart, be happy and change your life, you will have to choose it.

Define your life by what you give, not by what you have.

Entitlement is a suppressive trap, the attitude of being owed something, ego's clever feedback pointing you away from a heart-centered path.

Originating from fear, entitlement is a dense web of false beliefs, a magician's sleight-of-hand illusion, misdirecting you away from what your heart knows is real and true.

Entitlement is another form of resistance to your heart's calling; more feedback demonstrating the ego's feeble attempt to control the universe. Your heart understands the benefit of serving humanity, while the ego believes you are entitled to humanity serving you.

Feeling entitled is the misguided belief you have the right to something, usually at the expense of something or someone else. An ego-filled mind fears that if you don't get what you're entitled to, you will be made smaller and diminished, which to the ego represents death.

The secret code word for spotting when you are stuck in entitlement is "fair," as in, "That's not fair!" When you catch yourself making choices based on a reaction to something perceived as not fair, there's a good chance you're under entitlement's control.

At our company, entitlement ran rampant in the fall when our ranks filled with new college graduates. Because of prior successes from summer internships, graduating from top schools with honors, and coming from well-intentioned families that praised every effort, new employees, fresh to the work place, believed they were entitled to the best engagements, access to our high profile clients, and first-class travel to exotic locations.

It wasn't long before the truly talented teams realized their limitations, dropped their arrogance, and adopted a more down-to-earth, heart-centered service approach to their work, which counter-intuitively gained them higher favor with both superiors and clients.

Feeling entitled is a power trip with no real power. Expressing entitlement may give you a cause to defend, but by its nature, will result in your standing alone. Privately, leaders tell me, "I'm entitled to people's respect!"

Really? Why? Because you're the star of the show, or your title is chief executive officer or prime minister?

Far too often, when things don't go just right, I'll witness a famous person berate a service provider with a, "Do you know who I am?" Anyone, especially a celebrity or notable, looks small defending his or her perceived importance.

I am told the American singer Dolly Parton was flying first class, and a female fan in coach tried to make her way up the aisle to get a picture and autograph from Dolly. The head female flight attendant stopped the woman, saying, "Miss Parton is entitled to her privacy, please go back to your seat." Dolly turned around and sweetly instructed the flight attendant, "Miss, if it's okay with you, please let her up. If it wasn't for her, I wouldn't be sitting up here."

Choose less entitlement.

# Service

*I don't know what your destiny will be, but one thing I know:*
*The only ones among you who will be really happy*
*are those who have sought and found how to serve.*
*– Albert Schweitzer*

It is impossible to follow your heart, experience happiness and fulfill your life's purpose without consciously choosing a path that includes some form of daily service.

You were born to serve, arriving on this planet as an integral part of a holistically connected and synchronistic universe. In every moment, on more levels than you are aware, your life is an act of service. It doesn't matter if you are unaware or unwilling to serve. By the nature of your existence, by the choices you make, whether in thought or action, how you choose to serve this moment changes the future.

Serving this moment may mean you listen more than you speak.

Serving this moment may mean you volunteer your time, donate your money, share your insight, lend a hand, open your heart, or simply apologize.

Serving this moment may mean you walk away, or stay longer.

Serving this moment may mean you hold the hug, write another page of instruction, say a prayer, or follow your breath.

Serving this moment may mean you serve the Lord, serve the earth, serve humanity, serve your family, serve your community, or serve yourself.

Serving this moment may mean you hold yourself back and do absolutely nothing, or that you get on the plane, fly around the world, and spend the next six months teaching children to read.

*Your life, from before your first breath, to long after you are physically gone, is one grand act of service.*

If you truly want to understand your life's purpose here on earth, if your intention is to experience happiness, joy, peace and fulfillment, if you are committed to changing your life for the better, then you must get in the habit of consciously and directly asking the universe, "How may I serve you?"

*Everybody can be great . . . because anybody can serve. You don't have to have a college degree to serve. You don't have to make your subject and verb agree to serve. You only need a heart full of grace. A soul generated by love.*
*– Dr. Martin Luther King Jr.*

In Christianity, Ephesian 6:7 says, "Serve wholeheartedly, as if you were serving the Lord, not men." Islam teaches, "The best of men are those who are useful to others." And in the Church of Jesus Christ of Latter-day Saints, Book of Mormon, Mosiah 2.17, ". . . when you are in the service of your fellow beings you are only in the service of your God."

Your breath, insight, intuition, work, contributions, time, thoughts, experiences and creativity are all in service to some aspect of the whole. Without you, nothing – absolutely nothing – in your world would be the same. Your life, and how you choose to serve this moment, influences all of existence.

All service – all life – flows from this present moment. Your conscious choice is to either resist your heart's calling, living in fear and separation from others, or follow your heart and live free, happy and connected to all.

If you choose to serve from the ego, your thoughts will be, "What can I get?"

Choosing to serve from your heart, your feelings will always be, "What more can I give?"

Choose more service.

# Unlimited Possibilities

Whether you realize it or not, your existence guides the universe.

What you've achieved, the scenery around you, the people in your life, everything in this very moment, is the culmination, the apex of your choices. From this place, this exact moment in time, your next breath is the result of every decision you've ever made, and astonishingly influences every choice going forward.

When you own your power of choice, simple things that before were rote and mostly unconscious, become mystical and alive. Relationships, although always transitory, now extend beyond the boundaries of time, and true love begins permeating your connection to all living things. Everything in your world now, and in the future, is a result of your intentional, conscious decisions to either follow your heart, or not.

Indian-Bengali Nobel laureate, Rabindranath Tagore, said, "You can't cross the sea merely by standing and staring at the water."

In all subsequent moments, your life will grow in genuine meaning, direction and purpose, if you consciously become both the creator and attractor of your life's experience, owning this role with dignity and exuberance.

Wellness, love, work and play all become sacred, as your life becomes a compassionate act of service, filled with shades of awareness and kindness. No longer limited to fears, resistance or thoughts of failure, by acknowledging your heart's growing passions and excitement, and intentionally making each moment better, you become aligned to a grander function.

In each moment, your choices possess enormous power. Yet to follow your heart, be happy and change your life, none of this matters until you test the theory.

# One Less. One More.
# Steps

1. Start now.
2. Come present.
3. Consciously choose to follow your heart, be happy and change slowly.
4. Today, choose one less negative, resistant, or bad feeling thought or action, resulting in making the next moment worse.
   One Less: Worse.
5. Today, choose one more positive or good feeling thought or action, resulting in mak ing the next moment better.
   One More: Better.
6. Celebrate your progress.
7. Repeat tomorrow.

# Ten

---

## Mastery

**Less:** Perfection
**More:** Practice

> *If people knew how hard I*
> *had to work to gain my mastery,*
> *it wouldn't seem wonderful at all.*
> – *Michelangelo*

**I had a difficult time** finishing *One Less. One More.*

I wanted this last chapter of my first book to be perfect.

I was excited being so close to completing the work, and I wanted everything in perfect order. I diligently collected my notes, carefully reviewed the chapter's theme, examined my intention for the sub-headings, meticulously studied my interviews, labored over the outline, and conscientiously chose the appropriate case studies, making sure the chapter's foundation was strongly in place. Once I began writing, I thoughtfully crafted the lead and methodically went to work finishing the book.

And then, I got stuck. I began doubting myself,

sweating and second guessing the fine points, spending days writing and then rewriting the chapter's opening, reworking paragraphs, deleting sections, and changing everything so the end to *One Less. One More.* would be flawless.

Listening to the voices in my head, I worried, wondered, about all the things I was afraid would deter or derail me from finishing the book, and then, even worse, I agonized about dealing with future problems once the book was complete.

I stood paralyzed, and it wasn't long before I started losing sleep.

Although my job is helping people gain control of their lives, I clearly wasn't listening to my own counsel. Becoming angry with myself for not handling this better, I started projecting my frustration on family and friends. The harder I tried making this final chapter iron clad and perfect, the less fun I had, the more strained my writing became, and the further I was from finishing the book, which felt both disturbing and scary.

I had come all this way to follow my heart and write a book, only to become creatively constipated approaching the finish line.

Feeling tremendously out of sorts, I swallowed my pride, and asked my wife, Candace, for her guidance.

Candace sat me down at our kitchen table and calmly asked, "What's the theme of your last chapter?"

"Mastery," I replied. "Rejecting the illusion of perfection, and instead, embracing every moment as an opportunity to practice following your heart."

"Sounds like you solved the problem," Candace said, smiling. "Take your own advice: Stop trying to write the perfect book. Take a deep breath, celebrate that you're so close to finishing the work, and continue writing from your heart. Allow yourself the wonder of not knowing how the book's going to turn out, and have fun."

She was right.

I was caught in the illusion of attaining perfection. Stuck in an overwhelming cycle of fear and resistance, I was blocking myself from the present moment inspiration, passion and enthusiasm I needed to finish the book.

Once I let go of trying to create a work of perfection, came present, and consciously chose to enjoy the emerging process, I returned to the joy of creating. Almost immediately, I felt the weight of the world lift from my shoulders, and went on to complete *One Less. One More.*

# Less Perfection

*Have no fear of perfection – you'll never reach it.*
*– Salvador Dalí*

Perfection is unattainable, an impossible goal, another brilliant ruse by the ego to provide opposing feedback for following your heart. Like a dog chasing its tail, pursuing perfection is a dizzying distraction and never feels good.

You will never have perfect hair, a perfect day, perfect children, a perfect party, relationships, jobs, stocks, bosses, or a perfect fitness workout.

Gardens, shopping trips, golf swings, countries, meals and prayers cannot be perfect. Leadership is always flawed. Addiction recovery, teaching, financial independence, travel and optimum health cannot end in perfection; it's just not possible.

You cannot become a perfect Christian, Jew, Muslim, Buddhist, or Hindu. There are no perfect parents. You cannot be a perfect lover or friend. Your marriage will never be perfect. You cannot design the perfect house, write the perfect novel, or create the perfect business.

*If your goal is perfection, drop it now. Perfection is a trap, a dead end.*

Acknowledging their human imperfections, Native American Navajo weavers create every original handmade rug and blanket with a noticeable flaw, a tribute to the "Great Spirit," which in their belief system is the only place perfection exists.

Now, on the road to life mastery – reacting less to the world around you, and instead, consciously creating more of your heart's desire – it's time to wean yourself from the illusion of perfection.

The word "perfect" originates from the Latin word, *"perfectus,"* to be completed without flaw. Think of that: Completion with no flaws.

Imagine one day waking up thinking, "I'm done. I have no flaws and my life is complete. This is it, I'm finished and I'm perfect. I can die right now because there's nothing more to do."

I don't think so.

At the London world premiere of the twenty-third James Bond movie, *Skyfall*, director Sam Mendes was asked if he loves the film. He replied, "I never love any of my movies at this stage. Hate is probably closer to it, because you're so used to it and you see only its flaws. But I am very, very proud of it."

Tomorrow would not exist if you or the universe were perfect. Everything would stop right here. There would be nothing more to transform, discover, resolve or complete. If life were perfect, there would be nothing more to understand, to do, to become, or to express.

*The thing that is really hard, and really amazing, is giving up on being perfect and beginning the work of becoming yourself.*
*– Anna Quindlen*

For years, my running partner was friend, Eli Zabar, New York City-based master baker and culinary entrepreneur. During our early morning runs through New York's Central Park, Eli spoke passionately about his vision and devotion to the culinary world.

Our conversations were always about food, spanning the merits of pure, locally sourced, extra virgin olive oil, to the delicate nature of Peruvian chocolate, from the joys of an open food market in the south of France, to the pleasures of growing organic produce. We talked about fine wine, the delicate science of cheese, or that "lox," – as in my absolute favorite breakfast of lox and bagels – comes from the Yiddish word for salmon, *laks*.

One morning, during a glorious springtime run, we discussed the complexities of crafting and commercially distributing freshly baked artisanal bread, and I casually asked Eli if he considered himself a perfectionist?

"I am a perfectionist," he said, "and that will be the death of me. All bakers strive for the perfect loaf of bread, knowing in our hearts it doesn't exist. It's difficult for me to keep still or relax knowing that, although my customers may be happy, I continue falling short of my own personal, illusive goal of perfection."

# Recognizing Perfection's Trap

Here's a tip: Listen to your thoughts and conversations for the word "enough," as in, "I'm not good enough," or "I didn't do enough," or "You didn't try hard enough," and it's a safe bet you're caught in perfection's noose.

Which feels better?

The ego says, "Don't bother applying, you're not smart enough to get in here."

Your heart says, "You have the grades and this school feels just right. Submit your application."

The ego says, "You don't have enough money or time to travel."

Your heart says, "Save your money, make the time, and travel everywhere."

The ego says, "You're not creative enough."

Your heart says, "Design jewelry. Create pottery. Write a song. Tell jokes."

The ego says, "You're not compassionate enough."

Your heart says, "Become a social worker."

The ego says, "People will laugh at you. You're not talented enough."

Your heart says, "Act. Act in community theatre, act in student films, audition for commercials. Act!"

The ego says, "Who are you to teach anyone? You're not spiritual enough."

Your heart says, "Inspire humanity."

The ego says, "You don't have enough of what it takes."

Your heart says, "Serve your country."

The ego says, "You don't have enough patience to raise children."

Your heart says, "Have children."

The ego says, "You don't know enough to make that decision. Listen to your mother."

Your heart says, "It's okay if you don't have children."

The ego says, "I haven't accomplished enough to deserve being happy."

Your heart says, "You were born. That's enough. Be happy."

The ego says, "I'm not good enough for him/her."
Your heart says, "Ask him/her on a date."

Your fears are, "I'm not good enough."
Your heart knows, "I am enough, and more."

Remember, when you consciously choose to be happy and align with your life's true purpose, the ego acts a counter-weight, persistently trying to knock you off balance.

Once you become conscious of the ego as a feedback mechanism, you will never again allow yourself to feel bad for not being perfect. From the ego's flawed perspective, you are separate and disconnected from the universe, never being or having enough of anything. Recognize that although the ego relentlessly strives for perfection, always falling short of its goal, you can choose to feel good and follow your heart, knowing that perfection doesn't exist.

*Set your sights high and be all you can be, but remember, perfection is not a goal, and perfection is not productive.*
*– Douglas Alnwick, Pierson High School teacher,*
*Sag Harbor, NY*

It's easy buying into the "practice makes perfect" myth, because on the surface, perfection seems rational and appropriate when dedicated to winning and success. Yet, no matter what you do, pursuing perfection is futile.

Many over-achiever, Type A personalities pride themselves with the label, "perfectionist." Outwardly, they publicly criticize others, while privately berating themselves, defending their obsession as a requirement for success.

"Winners strive for perfection," new clients often say, believing perfection is the benchmark for victory. They are wrong.

Pursue excellence. Be all you can be in each moment. Endeavor to exceed expectations. Go beyond perceived limitations. Reach for the stars.

Just remember, though, striving for perfection *always* results in failure.

## It's Okay Being Wrong

For many years, I've advised a distinguished California winemaking family.

Now in their third generation of producing extraordinary wines, Jayden,\* the grandfather, who started the initial vineyard, was always competitively driven to produce the best wines in the world, regardless of the physical, emotional or financial consequences to his personal or professional life.

As the company grew, Jayden passed on his passion for perfection to his only son, Arthur,\* who then, over time, attempted imparting that same obsession to his only son, Phillip.\*

When Phillip took over the family's main vineyard, he attempted to follow in his father and grandfather's footsteps, portraying the image of a tough and obstinate vintner driven to perfection. As trained by his grandfather, Phillip acted like he was always in complete control, refusing to ask a question he didn't already know the answer to.

"You're in charge," grandfather Jayden roared. "Now act that way!"

For many years, Phillip felt depressed and terribly alone, believing if he didn't do everything perfectly, exactly as his grandfather and father had taught him, he would fail miserably, dishonor his family, and be responsible for driving the business into the ground.

Although Phillip loves winemaking, and the collaborative process of producing and selling a 100 percent pure agricultural product, "the spirit of the grape," as he calls it, Phillip confided that he could no longer lead the company – or as his father Arthur taught, "rule the brand" – in what many considered, a bully mentality. To save his soul, Phillip told me he was considering the unthinkable: leaving the family business.

One evening, after entertaining a group of visiting international wine journalists, Phillip and I headed along the dark, dirt path back to the main house, cautiously winding our way through the family's vineyard. Glancing up, I caught myself gasping at the countless stars in the brilliant night sky.

"What's wrong?" Phillip asked.

"Wrong?" I said in awe. "Nothing's wrong. Just look up!"

Phillip stopped, dropped his head, and said, "I'm sorry to admit, I never look up at the night sky."

"Why?" I asked.

"Because I feel like a phony," Phillip admitted. "Looking up at the stars reminds me how small and trivial I am, and that maybe I really don't know anything. Here I am running this multi-million dollar winery. I'm supposed to know it all, and I don't know crap."

"Really?" I asked rhetorically. "So tell me, how many planets are in our solar system?"

"Nine," Phillip replied quizzically.

"More or less," I said. "And how many solar systems are in our galaxy, the Milky Way?"

Thinking a moment, he answered, "I don't know."

"Approximately one hundred billion," I told him. "And tell me, how many galaxies do you think are in what scientists call the 'Observable Universe?'"

Pausing, Phillip replied in a sad whisper, "I have no idea."

"Another one hundred billion," I said.

"And what does this mean to me?" Phillip asked, in what was becoming an angry tone.

"It means your grandfather was wrong," I said. "When you do the math and multiply the nine planets in one solar system, with another one hundred billion solar systems in our galaxy, with another one hundred billion or so galaxies in the universe, and all the knowledge that could be contained within those systems, it becomes clear that nobody really knows anything compared to all there is to know."

"And . . .?" Phillip probed further.

"Perfection doesn't exist," I said. "If it did, the universe would stop right here. It's okay – normal, really – not knowing everything. It's okay learning from your mistakes. It's okay being in awe. It's okay asking questions. It's okay being wrong."

"Go on," Phillip told me.

"It's not only okay, but it's fun being vulnerable and leading a world class team with an exciting vision," I explained. "And, more important, it's okay to build this vineyard from your heart."

At breakfast the following morning, I suggested to Phillip that at least once every day he consciously stop himself from trying to oversee the vineyard in the hard intimidating style of his father and grandfather, and instead, slow down, take a deep breath, and simply observe the results of his not being a tyrant.

"That's your daily one less," I said.

I also suggested that at least once a day, Phillip practice following his heart; allowing himself the luxury of exploring his childhood dream of building a wine company that expresses reverence for the soul of every grape, while also placing value on each life involved with producing every bottle of wine.

"That's your daily one more," I said.

Both Phillip and his winery continued thriving. Soon after our talk, Phillip broke with family tradition, and asked his chief winemaker a relatively naïve question, one that grandfather Jayden would have called "stupid."

"Wow," the chief winemaker said, "I don't know the answer to that either, but it seems so simple, let's try it."

From that one innocuous question came the innovation for a wildly popular and profitable new line of white wines that continues winning industry awards, along with critical and consumer praise.

Perfection only exists in the moment. You can experience perfection, but you cannot create it, nor can you accurately express it.

Perfection is not a form of life. You cannot find perfection, you cannot create perfection, you will not earn perfection, and nothing you do will ever bring you any closer to the mirage of perfection.

Originating from ego's feedback system, perfection is an arbitrary concept based on artificial rules, regulations, standards, guidelines, estimations and protocols, with no counterpart in nature.

Imagine an apple, raccoon, cloud, snowflake, the moon, a tree, piece of coral, your pet, a molecule of DNA, or the ocean trying to be perfect.

*Art is never finished, only abandoned.*
*– Leonardo da Vinci*

An artist may experience truth in the perfection of a winter's sunset, or a falling teardrop, sleeping cat, rusty nail, or snowcapped mountain, yet she may die trying unsuccessfully to express that perfection in her paintings.

*You do not lower your standards or let anyone down if you stop pursuing perfection. Instead, the nobler pursuit is to be fulfilled, happy, peaceful, compassionate, aligned with your life's purpose, and to experience countless perfect moments.*

Instead of complying to the ego's constant unachievable demand to, "Be perfect," over time, you'll recognize the feedback and consciously flip to your heart's loving suggestion to, "Just be."

Less perfection. More practice.

# Practice More Gratitude

*The essence of all beautiful art, all great art, is gratitude.*
*– Friedrich Nietzsche.*

Practice living in gratitude. Learn to experience life from the heart, viewing your world in universal light, seeing each moment without the fog of fear, without illusion, without judgment.

Gratitude is blind to the superficial, temporal, obvious and the mundane, instead, celebrating each moment as a divine gift possessing the potent seeds of unlimited possibilities.

The language of gratitude consists of only two words, "Thank you." And when you stop, come present and begin practicing more gratitude, the ego has no choice but to become quiet in the emerging awareness of your heart's expansion.

Beyond the reaches of conscious awareness, gratitude illuminates inconceivable webs of synchronicities, which, ultimately, creates the framework for your physical world. In the eyes of the universe, practicing gratitude makes you more obvious, bigger and brighter as you continue experiencing your heart's dreams and desires.

More than a psychological exercise, practicing gratitude is a form of prayer, an expressive, meditative function for giving thanks; recognizing that each moment-to-moment experience is, indeed, an exquisite gift.

Choosing more gratitude is protective, a celestial form of insurance against gloom and despair.

Consider, for example, if you did nothing but express gratitude for your physical, beating heart:

Within a month of your conception, your heart, the first organ to begin forming in your emerging body, has already begun beating blood through the embryo. And once born, your heart will beat an average of one hundred and ten thousand times per day, and more than three billion times over the course of a normal life span.

Your heart, which sends more information to your brain than your brain sends to your heart, is one hundred times electrically, and possibly five thousand times magnetically, stronger than your brain.

You've chosen to follow your heart, be grateful for its magnificence.

Once you gain gratitude for your heart, don't stop

there. Consider the countless ways of expressing gratitude for your miraculous body, your own material power plant. How lucky are you to taste food, smell a flower, hold your children, weep for a loss, gasp at a shooting star, or feel the soft fur of a recently born pup.

Have you ever stopped to consider the mechanics, chemistry and neurological functions of a kiss? Or, how a cut heals? Or a bone mends? Or how over one trillion active good bacteria productively work in your gut? Be grateful for your body.

Now keep going.

Be grateful for your family, friends, relatives, ancestors and all humanity.

Give thanks to the police for keeping you safe. Give thanks to the garbage men, tollbooth clerks, street cleaners, hospital workers and soldiers standing post to protect our freedom. Give thanks for your leaders, teachers, neighbors, bosses, postal workers, restaurant service staff, ferryboat operators, park rangers and countless more. Look for more ways to give thanks. Even strangers are blessed when you smile at them in gratitude.

In our home, before we eat, we express gratitude by saying, "Dear Creator, thank you for this food, its preparer and its source. Thank you that we can share this meal together, in this moment, and we bless this food, as it nourishes and blesses our body, and for anything that gave its life so that we may be fed, we are eternally grateful."

If you want to feel bad, place your attention on what you don't have. Conversely, to feel good, practice becoming grateful for everything in your life.

The challenge, of course, is seeing light and beauty through the corporeal forms of mistakes, labels, perceptions, beliefs, positions, disapproval, prejudice, hatred, ignorance and grief, and still be grateful.

Practice gratitude for all your problems, health issues, crisis, difficult finances, lost jobs, faltering relationships and concerns, because hidden beyond your anger, resentment, bitterness and fears, is the door to your awakening, the path to peace.

Becoming proficient in gratitude takes time. Take it slow. Consciously catch yourself in any given moment, and find something – many things – for which you can practice and express gratitude. Over time, it will become effortless. Expressing gratitude demonstrates the shift, the fulcrum of your personal transformation into life mastery. Practice more gratitude.

# Practice More Forgiveness

To settle an ugly labor dispute, the CEO, Brian,* was forced by his board to fire the company's number two executive, Jack.*

Jack, a smart, nimble leader, swiftly used the crisis to his advantage, and with his non-compete clause voided, founded a new company in direct competition to Brian's business. Jack's company was soon thriving.

Brian was furious. He saw Jack's success as a personal affront, and wanted Jack's new company destroyed.

Over the following months, Brian became obsessed with

Jack's success, which began shackling his own leadership.

In session, I asked Brian for his personal and business goals over the following twelve to eighteen months.

Along with growing his company and expanding into South America, Brian wanted to spend more time with his wife and children, speak enough Japanese to impress his colleagues in Kyoto, complete a one hundred-mile bike ride, and write poetry.

I asked, "How is destroying Jack's company helping you achieve those goals?"

Quick to defend, Brian replied, "I just can't let him get away with this!"

I asked Brian to consider practicing forgiveness.

"Catch yourself at least once a day feeling resentment or anger toward Jack," I told him. "Consciously pivot away from the ego's negative feelings of revenge, and to better see the larger picture, choose the filter of compassion."

I also suggested Brian make a daily decision to follow his heart and passions, enthusiastically pursuing more of his personal goals, which included taking his kids to school and training on his bike.

It only took a week before I got the call.

"What the heck am I doing?" Brian said over the phone. "Am I insane? Jack's a good guy, there's room for both of us in the space and, although my efforts aren't hurting Jack, my blood pressure is up, I've become distracted, and I'm just wasting time!"

Within a year, Brian achieved all his goals except speaking Japanese, and, as the universe works, on a trans-

Atlantic flight, he found himself sitting next to Jack in first class, resulting in a renewed friendship and a very successful joint venture.

Forgiveness is the final obstacle, the last test of life mastery.

Forgiveness is the act of consciously choosing to experience each moment more from your heart than your head.

This will forever be the benchmark for life mastery:

Will you, can you, under any circumstance, at any point in your life, recognize when the fear-based and limiting ego is in control, and consciously pivot to an experience more from your heart?

Forgiveness is not something to give away or bestow on someone else.

True forgiveness is a gift you give yourself.

Neither perfect nor absolute, practicing forgiveness is a lifelong process often fraught with pain and resistance.

Like X-ray vision, forgiveness sees through ego's false illusions of separation, and instead, experiences each moment, every situation, as whole, connected and infinite.

But to feel forgiveness, you must choose it.

So, how will you choose?

How will you treat yourself after you gain five pounds during the holiday?

How will you act when someone bumps into you on the subway or the bus?

What will you do when a car quickly pulls out ahead of you, or someone cuts the line at the gas station, or a group of teenagers flips you off?

How long will you feel bad after you fail the test, get dumped, passed over for promotion, or your new stock purchase goes the wrong way?

How will you handle being ridiculed for still being a virgin, short, bald, handicapped, single, or eccentric?

What are your choices after your spouse cheats, your partner lies, your parents condemn you, or all your children forget your birthday?

What's your next step after discovering corruption in the government, a bad cop, waste in the budget, a mistake in the blueprints, or a misdiagnosis?

You cannot think your way through forgiveness, just as you can't think your way through darkness. Illumination – light – is the only antidote for navigating the shadows, and true forgiveness only comes from the heart.

Saying, "I forgive you," means you have consciously chosen to experience a person or situation more from your open heart, and less from a closed mind. And just saying, "I forgive you," doesn't make it so until you feel it from your heart.

From the head, forgiveness is always a reaction; from the heart, forgiveness is a compassionate response, the choice of life mastery.

My clients often ask:

How do you forgive perpetrators, thieves, liars, cheats, scoundrels, crooks, villains and criminals?

How is it possible to truly forgive heinous, evil actions?

How do you forgive a rapist, a predator, or a mass

murderer?

How do you forgive someone for breaking your heart?

How do you forgive a nation, a corporation, a financial institution, or a race of people for crimes against humanity?

My reply is always the same: Healing begins the instant you observe anything, even evil, more from your heart than the head, which is really the only choice you have in any given moment. Choosing forgiveness does not mean you accept or condone a person or their actions; it simply means you consciously shift to a more heart-centered experience, and less to the perils and drama of the ego.

There is no right or wrong process for forgiveness, no shortcut or set of tricks. I've never been able to counsel any client on a standard forgiveness protocol, or set of rules or tips to follow when forgiveness is required.

To fulfill your life's purpose and be happy, you must practice forgiveness, the conscious and physical act of experiencing any moment, regardless how uncomfortable or unpleasant, more from your heart than the feedback of ego.

People do some pretty terrible, ugly, nasty and stupid things. Truth is, so do we. You can't change the past. You can only change your intentions, thoughts and actions now.

The ego wants to blame and stay angry, which is unhealthy and counter-productive. Holding in rage, fury, revenge, irritation, wrath, anger, and other negative feelings, ultimately leads to pain, dis-ease, and possible early death. There is an ancient Chinese proverb, "He who seeks vengeance must dig two graves; one for his enemy, and one for himself." Seeking revenge is like taking poison every day hoping the other person will get sick and die. You create the future. Choose wisely. Practice more forgiveness.

# Practice More

*We are Buddhists, not Buddha. That's why we need practice.*
*– Gelek Rimpoche*

Here's the reality:

All of this, every concept in this book, is just a premise; ideas told through a filter, a prism, the limitations of my words, beliefs, opinions and experiences.

I write what I believe is true, yet until *you* consciously choose to change your life, come present and act on following your heart, the words and principles in this book remain static theory.

I am just a guy with a simple idea for changing your life and being happy: the slow and sustainable transformation of following your heart – One Less, One More – which in my experience, continues yielding remarkable results across geographical boundaries, cultures and religions. But One Less, One More only works because each person, individually, took this theoretical information and applied it to their own personal practice.

Life mastery is simply the conscious daily commitment to being happy, following your heart, letting go of anything not aligned to your life's purpose, and continually discovering more of what is.

The more you practice One Less, One More, the more you will experience the infinite possibilities available to you in this moment, today, tomorrow and forever.

Your potential is unfathomable, your creativity unlimited and your capacity for love, joy, health and success, unmatched by anything you know in your present life. The universe does not support lack.

Out of more than seven billion people on this planet, awakening to changing your life and becoming happy will always be in your own time, at your own pace, through whatever means keeps you aligned with following your heart.

Don't bother looking around to see if what you're doing is correct, because the experience of following your heart, and the subsequent journey to becoming happy and aligning with your life's purpose, is so deeply personal and unique, that for now and forever, this singular path will only be appropriate for one person: *You.*

One Less, One More works, but only when you consciously choose to show up, observe ego's feedback without engaging in the fear, drama, resistance, or illusion, and continually practice the often-hard work required for achieving your goals, dreams and desires.

There is no perfection, silver bullet, Fountain of Youth, lucky charm, magic potion, shortcuts, or easy answers to life's uncertainties. One Less, One More holds no ageless secrets or veiled truths. For you to consciously embrace your life's journey, as uncomfortable as it may feel at times, requires a constant, unwavering belief in the elegance of slow, incremental and sustainable change.

On this heart-centered path, and for the rest of your life, you, too, will fail, fall, slip and regress. Accept that conflict and resistance are okay; just part of the adventure. Every crisis, large and small, *always* results in transformation and change, and it's what you do with that change that matters. Remember, if you fall, just get back up one more time, and the setback is temporary.

*Without setbacks and mistakes, no experience. Without experience, no learning. And without learning, you'll never truly understand the awakening of your heart's desires.*

Choose to be conscious and aware in every moment, and continue focusing on how you feel, not what you have or haven't achieved. Be kind and stop beating yourself up. Stop keeping score.

Practice getting in touch with your extraordinary feedback system, and when you're feeling bad, do something about feeling good. Choose to make the moment better. And with kind, loving patience, compassionately come back into alignment with your life's purpose. Treat yourself and others with the intention of making things better, not worse.

Until you choose to follow your heart and pursue your dreams, you will never understand your astonishing purpose in life. Until you begin a daily practice, and take the first steps into the unknown, everything remains just theory.

Professional athletes practice more than they play. Olympians practice their entire lives for one brief feat. And first responders practice daily for events they hope never happen.

You may want to play piano, guitar, or xylophone, and, in fact, take lessons, but the real work, the true growth, the mastery comes in the continued practice; not the theory.

You weren't born a remarkable parent; it's something you become after years of daily practice.

Going to karate class, tennis camp, golf lessons, or driving school doesn't make you a master, practice does.

Becoming a more observant Jew, or following Jesus, Buddha, or Mohammad, is just the beginning of your spiritual journey. What truly matters is how in each moment, over the course of your life, you practice, experience and express Christianity, Judaism, Islam, or Buddhism, every day.

Choosing to start a non-profit organization, digital media company, summer camp, new school, or small business, isn't enough. To become successful, you must practice and stick with your business and leadership principles every day.

Creating a budget is a good idea, although practicing control of your finances creates sound fiscal responsibility.

Either write your book, movie, poem, blog or article, or don't. But until you start practicing your writing, it will never get better, regardless of the outcome.

Want better sex? Practice.

Want to be more grateful, loving, kind, giving, open

and happy? Practice.

Want to change the world? Practice self-love, and the world will change with you.

Recovering from a terrible injury, illness, war injury, disease or accident doesn't come through theory. Healing is a daily spiritual, physical and emotional practice that requires time, patience and support.

Want to conquer your fears? Practice.

You don't kick an addiction because you simply make the choice. It requires daily practice for the rest of your life, period.

During the time it took me to complete this book, I contracted Lyme Disease, had heart surgery, experienced a devastating financial blow during the global recession, lost one of my best friends, several friends divorced, people I cared for lost their home, and our oldest child left for college, soon to be followed by his sister.

Through it all, I had only two choices: Do I resist life, feel bad and become a victim to circumstances? Or, do I practice what I preach, come present, let go, choose to be happy and, regardless of the situation, continue following my heart?

I chose to embrace my beautiful life, take one day at a time, spend abundant time with my family, friends and pets, passionately follow my heart, have fun, grow closer to all humanity and nature, consciously choose less of what makes me feel bad, while at the same time, discovering and experiencing more of what feels good.

I encourage you to join me and do the same.

# Practice One Less, One More

Every day, let go of at least one thought or experience that doesn't feel good and not aligned with your heart's calling. And, in the same day, choose more ways to follow your heart, be happy, do what you love, and enthusiastically and passionately change your life.

Believe you were born to be happy.

Commit daily to following your heart and fulfilling your dreams and desires.

Confidently, let go of trying to control the outcome of your life, and instead, trust the universe will readily and joyfully fulfill your intentions.

Fearlessly make the changes today you want to see in the world tomorrow.

Take full responsibility for your life. Become accountable for your existence.

Choose in each moment to make things better, not worse.

Practice forgiveness. Practice gratitude.

Drop the idea of perfection, and instead, live each moment filled with abundance, passion, fun, joy, peace, harmony, beauty, service and love.

Go now. Leave these words and abandon the theory.

Come present.

Take a few slow, deep breaths.

Courageously choose to follow your heart and be happy.

Know in your heart-of-hearts that it is okay to change slowly.

Engage your dreams and desires.

Rise higher.

Serve others.

Embrace and experience your magnificent, glorious, transformation.

Remember: Your life matters, and we are all in this together.

One Less. One More.

# One Less. One More.
# Steps

1. Start now.
2. Come present.
3. Consciously choose to follow your heart, be happy and change slowly.
4. Today, choose one less thought or action in the futile pursuit of perfection and let it go.
   One Less: Perfection.
5. Today, practice one more thought or action focused on achieving your heart's dreams and desires.
   One More: Practice.
6. Practice forgiveness and gratitude. Celebrate your life!
7. Repeat tomorrow.

# The Daily
# One Less, One More
# Moment

Dear Universal Creator,

I choose to be happy, do what I love, and follow my heart. I am present and prepared for the challenge.

I am aligned with my life's purpose, and without judgment, persistently observe the feedback my existence provides, consciously choosing to feel good, while honoring the natural process of slow, incremental, and sustainable change.

My life is the fulfillment of my heart's dreams and desires, and today I choose one less negative, resistant, fearful, or bad feeling, thought or action, and let it go.

Also today, I consciously choose one more positive, joyful, or good feeling, thought or action, and fully embrace it with all my being.

I know this as One Less, One More.

Now, in this moment, I celebrate my birth, my life, as an experience and expression of the universe's magnificence, and commit to making every conscious moment better than I found it.

I am happiness, love, and light.

All is well.

# Gratitude and Appreciation

I did not, nor could I, write this book alone.

I am grateful for my parents, Lawrence S. Vorhaus and Dr. Renee P. Vorhaus, my brother, William M. Vorhaus; and my two sisters, Lauren Adele Vorhaus and Elizabeth Carla Oz.

I am deeply grateful for Glorynn Ross and Irene Rebecca Bodendorf. Thank you for your loving and light-filled spiritual guidance and counsel. Also, thank you Sid and Grandma.

For opening my heart to the love and light of grace and goodness, along with sharing your time and compassion, I am grateful for the late Pope John Paul II, and The Most Reverend Desmond Tutu.

Although I cannot publicly acknowledge my clients, thank you for the profound honor of serving you, and for sharing my belief that truth is the ultimate spin.

Thank you, Lisa Chiovaro, for keeping me sane, honest and solvent. And for what it's worth, Ana Peres Flores was right.

I am blessed living in Sag Harbor, New York, our jewel by the sea. I am grateful for my entire community, and especially thankful for Colin Ambrose, Samantha and Greg Bradford, Carl Brandl, Edward Burke, Jr., Ted Conklin, Shannon D'Andrea, James DePasquale, James and Anne Dwoskin, Robert Evjen, Dan Hartnett, Blake Kerr, Missie Mahoney, Toby and Fred Marienfeld, Colin Mather, Tracy

**One Less. One More.**

Mitchell, Jeff Peters, Rich Terry, Chris Tice and Steve Cox, and especially, Brigette McMahon for the phone call that inspired me to write the original "One Less, One More" column for the *Sag Harbor Express*.

Thank you *Sag Harbor Express* for running the initial "One Less, One More – The Sag Harbor Effect" column, especially Bryan Boyhan, Gavin and Kathryn G. Menu, Annette Hinkle and Judy Clempner.

While writing *One Less. One More.* many people volunteered their precious time to read and comment on the manuscript, providing invaluable feedback and direction. Thank you Kevin Carroll, Raul Colon, Kelly Connaughton Dodds, Tom Grassano, Joan Koslow, Len Lollback, Helen Marino, Katherine Mitchell, Gordon Mott, Karen Neveu, Karen Pace, Mona Peláez, Erik Proulx, and Al Terry.

I am grateful to Doug Hirschhorn, who introduced me to my editor, Amy Hertz, who made a good book infinitely better. Thank you, too, Barbara Spence, for your meticulous proofreading and contribution to clarity.

I was lucky enough to write parts of *One Less. One More.* in Maine, San Francisco, London, Mumbai, Paris, and Dublin. Yet my favorite writing spot was watching the daily sunrise overlooking Pittwater Bay in Sydney, Australia. Thank you Mark, Alisa, Tallis, Kye, and Koda Lollback, along with the entire Lollback family; I love you dearly.

I am blessed with more friends than one human could ever hope for. For lifting me through this project (and my life), I thank Bonni K. Brodnick, John Cassillo, Rob

Gregory, Scott Griffith, Nancy Heiberg and Greg Houser, Dennis Lord, Marc and Agnes Lurton, Chuck Marino, Sophie and Hugues de'Montvallon, Matt Murray, Saul Mori Pressner, Nicolas Rousseaux and Yveline Renaud, Jerome Rousseaux, Eric and Stephanie Schnaible, Melissa Sukiennik, and Mara Williams.

I am also grateful to the entire Pearlfisher team for their brilliant creation of our One Less, One More brand image, especially, Mike Branson, Hamish Campbell, Tess Wicksteed and Teres Rodney.

Thank you, too, Amy Rose Grigoriou for your jacket design contribution, and Alan Hebel and Ian Koviak for your beautiful interior design. You are all book design masters.

And for championing our story, thank you Rusty Shelton and your incredible team at Shelton Interactive.

Lubbu to my best friend and life partner, Mary Candace Connors Vorhaus; and our two magnificent children, Connor William Vorhaus and Molly Gayle Vorhaus; I love you more than love itself. I also promised Molly I would acknowledge my four-legged writing partner, and bestest diggity dog ever, Oliver "Fa-Ching" Vorhaus.

And finally, thanks to *you*.

Consciously choosing to follow your heart, pursue your dreams, be happy and change your life is a Herculean task not to be taken lightly. And so, with deep gratitude and admiration, I humbly bow to your courageous journey. Namaste.